MYSTERIES
CONFUCIUS
COULDN'T SOLVE

MYSTERIES CONFUCIUS COULDN'T SOLVE

Analysis of Ancient Characters Reveal Intriguing Facts Shared with Hebrew Scriptures

Ethel R. Nelson and Richard E. Broadberry

READ BOOKS

Publisher

South Lancaster, MA

Published by Read Books Publisher, P.O. Box 776, S. Lancaster, MA 01561.

Printed in the United States of America.

Library of Congress Catalog Card Number: 86-90431

ISBN 0-937869-00-7

DEDICATION

To Kang Chong Heng, the one who first opened my eyes to the ancient Chinese world and the analysis of its fascinating ideographic characters. What an honor and pleasure to work with him in writing a prior book, *THE DISCOVERY OF GENESIS*, fragments of which are used in composing this new work. Although now aged, and unable to participate in this present endeavor, his influence lives on.

ETHEL R. NELSON

To my parents, Mr. & Mrs. N.E. Broadberry; Ron and Doreen Barber; Ray and Yvonne Rona; and Stephen Broadberry; for their love, prayers and encouragement.

RICHARD E. BROADBERRY

CONTENTS

ACKNOWLEDGMENTS

After scanning this book, you may feel that you need a good magnifying glass to read it! However, we have tried to alleviate this problem somewhat by enlarging the contained Chinese characters in the margins. Although some pages may look quite formidable to a non-Chinese readership because of the sprinkling of unfamiliar symbols, yet we have made the text easy to follow and before long, one will begin to recognize the ancient pictograms and even perhaps anticipate a meaning!

A previously published book, *The Discovery of Genesis* (Concordia), co-authored with C.H. Kang, has received some criticism, and probably rightfully so. Where it failed was in not going back to the most ancient Chinese character forms (Bronzeware and Oracle Bone inscriptions). This present work has done just this. Large numbers of the earlier written forms support the thesis that the ancient Chinese had a true knowledge of earth's beginnings. And we have barely scratched the surface in this book! As the study progressed, it has seemed more and more likely that much of the primitive Chinese writing was based upon their pristine sacred concepts, even as the Egyptians produced hieroglyphs, illustrating their religious tenets.

We are not claiming infallibility in our analysis of the characters, for as in any type of research, changes are bound to be made as understanding increases. However, it does seem that "the law of compound probability" is certainly at play and that mere coincidence can be ruled out by the hundreds of nicely integrated elements brought together in logical combinations. Comparison of ancient Chinese and Hebrew concepts of early earth history fits like a tongue-in-groove and helps gel a liquid hypothesis into a solid theory.

Studying these fascinating Chinese characters of antiquity kept me glued to my chair for hours at a time in rather lonely pursuit until enthusiastic and quizzical Richard Broadberry joined the "search and rescue" exercises. Although most of our sharing and working together has been by correspondence, we have each been stimulated by the other's ideas and finds.

I would like to thank Steven Lin for initially encouraging me to undertake this particular emphasis with a Chinese translation; David Lin for reviewing early phases of the work; Peggy Chau for lending her hand with tedious aspects of the study; my son-in-law and daughter, Dr. Gerard Damsteegt and Laurel, for advising on the manuscript; Pastor Richard Mendola for insisting on an English edition; Miss Wei Te Chen and Mr. Hsu Ching Chung for their help with our understanding of the Chinese textbooks used in our research; Mr. Edward Lien, publisher of the Living Stone Press, Taipei, for encouragement and use of his facilities; Mr. Kuang Yuan Chang for introducing the Oracle Bone inscriptions to us; Mr. Su Wen K'uei for his ancient character renditions in the chapter headings; and my trusty Canon word processor for helping me keep my sanity in the numerous revisions!

Mr. Chris Christianson's innovative, artistic ideas and talent seemed to lend just the right aura to the ancient *Sacrifice* portrayed by this Oracle Bone pictogram on the cover.

Use of a number of Scriptural versions seemed appropriate, and are identified in the references as: *King James Version* (KJV); *New King James Version* (NKJV); *New International Version* (NIV); *Today's English Version* (TEV); and the *Revised Standard*

Acknowledgments

Version (RSV).

It is hoped that any Chinese philologist who might chance to read this book may not think it too impertinent for two foreigners to invade this ancient precinct and attempt a "New Look at an Old Language" (see Epilog). We have suggested a number of "keys" to unlock the greatest mystery of all— that of interpreting what we believe is the true meaning behind many Chinese characters!

Ethel R. Nelson, M.D.
Dunlap, Tennessee

CHAPTER 1

THE RIDDLE

"He who understands the ceremonies of the sacrifices to Heaven and Earth, . . . would find the government of a kingdom as easy as to look into his palm!" Confucius, THE DOCTRINE OF THE MEAN, Ch. xix, 6.

For forty centuries the reigning emperors of China had traveled annually to the border of the country or imperial city. There, on an outdoor altar, they sacrificed and burned young unblemished bullocks to *ShangTi* (上帝), the "Heavenly Ruler."

The BORDER SACRIFICE, as it came to be called, was a ceremony conducted in unbroken sequence from the "legendary period" of Chinese history, even before the first dynastic rule beginning in 2205 B.C. This rite ended only in 1911 of our own century after a continual observance of more than 4,000 years! The Imperial SACRIFICE had become closely identified with the rulership of China, for the emperor himself was the chief participant in the ceremony. Consequently, when the Manchus were deposed in 1911, not only the dynastic reign ended forever, but also China's longest celebrated and most colorful BORDER SACRIFICE.

So important to the mind of the sage, Confucius (551-479 B.C.), was the Great SACRIFICE that he compared a comprehension of the ritual to the efficient ruling of the Chinese empire! YET HE, HIMSELF, COULD FIND NO REASON FOR THE SACRIFICE TO *SHANGTI,* WHICH REMAINED AN UNSOLVED RIDDLE. WHY DID CONFUCIUS ATTACH SO MUCH SIGNIFICANCE TO THIS MYSTERIOUS BORDER SACRIFICE?

Even the origins of the Sacrifices to Heaven and Earth are enigmatic. One of the earliest accounts is found in the *Shu Ching (Book of History,* compiled by Confucius) where it is recorded of Emperor *Shun* (c. 2230 B.C.) that "he sacrificed to *ShangTi.* "[1] This emphasizes MYSTERY NUMBER TWO: WHO IS *SHANGTI?*

In the 15th century A.D., the service was moved to the southern part of Peking where an extensive park came to quarter three main sacred edifices. In

1420, a great Hall of Prayer for Good Harvests was completed. This northern-most temple is mounted on a triple-tiered, white marble terrace with surrounding balustrades 11 meters (36 feet) high.

50,000 blue, glazed tiles (representing the sky) cover a cone-shaped roof, also three-tiered. No nails were used in the construction of the circular wall which is supported by 28 wooden columns hewn from single trees. In the center are four great pillars, which together with the outer framework, support the roof without the use of ceiling joists. The entire interior is painted in multi-color designs.

To the south is a second smaller Temple of Heaven, the Imperial Vault. Its plan follows the same architecture, except the blue-tiled roof is a single cone. INSIDE THIS EDIFICE RESIDES NO IDOL, but a tablet on the north wall is inscribed with the characters 皇天上帝 (Heavenly Sovereign *ShangTi*).

In a straight line, yet further south, is the altar of sacrifice itself. This great, triple-tiered, white marble Altar of Heaven, 75 meters (250 feet) in diameter, again surrounded on each level by balustrades, has the appearance of a gigantic wedding cake. The uppermost level can be reached by series of steps on each of four sides. A monumental undertaking, construction of it was completed in 1539.

Let us now transport ourselves backward in time

to observe, first-hand, the events surrounding ancient China's most sacred site and rite. As the winter solstice (about December 22) approaches, the supporting cast readies itself for the glorious ritual.

Singers prepare their colorful silken robes; musicians dust off their racks of suspended bronze bells, varying-sized drums, cymbals, flutes and stringed instruments, dedicated exclusively for use in this annual event.

On the morning before the winter solstice, the emperor, the "Son of Heaven" in gorgeous array, passes through the front gate of the Imperial Palace (the "Forbidden City") and makes his way in a procession to the Temple of Heaven park. An impressive retinue of princes and high officials follow. The streets of Peking are silent, as all residents are required to remain hidden behind shuttered windows.

By reviewing the litany of prayers and praises, one may begin to understand the Chinese attitude toward the Heavenly Being, *ShangTi.* After arriving at the Temple of Heaven, the emperor first meditates in the Imperial Vault while the costumed singers, accompanied by the musicians, sing the recitation:

> "To Thee, O mysteriously-working Maker, I look up in thought. How imperial is the expansive arch, (where Thou dwellest.) ... with the great ceremonies I reverently honour Thee. Thy servant, I am but a reed or willow; my heart is but as that of an ant;

yet have I received Thy favouring decree, appointing me to the government of the empire. I deeply cherish a sense of my ignorance and blindness, and am afraid lest I prove unworthy of Thy great favours. Therefore will I observe all the rules and statutes, striving, insignificant as I am, to discharge my loyal duty. Far distant here, I look up to Thy heavenly palace. Come in Thy precious chariot to the altar. Thy servant, I bow my head to the earth, reverently expecting Thine abundant grace. All my officers are here arranged along with me, joyfully worshipping before Thee ... Oh that Thou wouldest vouchsafe to accept our offerings, and regard us, while thus we worship Thee, whose goodness is inexhaustible! "[2]

The emperor then makes his way to the Hall of Prayer for Good Harvests.

On the morrow's festive solstice, the emperor returns to the Temple of Heaven Imperial Vault and then proceeds to the Altar of Heaven to perform the sacrificial rituals. The crisp morning air is filled with songs of praise and prayer. (Some of these will be presented at appropriate points in subsequent chapters). Gems and silks are brought forth, as well as vessels of food, and three offerings of wine, all accompanied by music and dances:

"The dances have all been performed, and nine times the music has resounded. Grant, O *Te* [*ShangTi*], Thy great blessing to increase the happiness of my house. The instruments of metal and precious stones have given out their melody. The jewelled girdles of the officers have emitted their tinklings . . . . While we celebrate His great name, what limit can there be, or what measure? For ever He setteth fast the high heavens, and establisheth the solid earth. His government is everlasting. His unworthy servant, I bow my head, I lay it in the dust, bathed in his grace and glory."[3]

As the sacrificial bullock is burned, a final song resounds:

"We have worshipped and written the Great Name on this gem-like sheet. Now we display it before *Te, [ShangTi]* and place it in the fire. These valuable offerings of silks and fine meats we burn also, with these sincere prayers, that they may ascend in volumes of flames up to the distant azure. All the ends of the earth look up to Him. All human beings, all things on the earth, rejoice together in the Great Name."[4]

Today the Temple and Altar of Heaven (*T'ien T'an*) in Peking are prime tourist attractions. Few people in the surging crowds that clamber over the worn marble steps even concern themselves with wondering about the origin and meaning of the "Great Sacrifice." Centuries ago, the obscure rite which inspired the construction of these cryptic edifices, captivated the imagination of Confucius, but even the sage had no answer to the riddle.

The Riddle

Is it possible that we can decipher the puzzle and trace the original intention of this magnificent ceremony of antiquity? We believe so—and by a most unusual means! We will find, too, strangely enough, that even though the ritual is no longer practiced in China today, it still has great significance for ALL—those of the Western world, as well as the Orient!

CHAPTER 2

WHO IS *SHANGTI*?

Chi lu asked . . . "I venture to ask about death?"
The Master answered . . . "While you do not know life, how can you know about death?" CONFUCIAN ANALECTS, Bk. xi, Ch. XI.

Do you ever wonder where you came from? Most people do. Do you have a well-kept family record of ancestors covering many generations? Regardless of whether or not you know who your ancestors were, do you have any idea how mankind and all life on earth came into being? Who were the very first human beings? Were they intelligent, or————?

Some scientists today tell us that mankind has

evolved through countless ages from lower forms of life. They say that man emerged as an upright creature, a descendant of an apelike animal. BUT DID YOU KNOW THAT THE ANCIENT TEACHINGS OF THE CHINESE REVEAL THAT THE FIRST MAN AND WOMAN ON EARTH WERE STATELY, INTELLIGENT, SPECIALLY CREATED BEINGS? They even resembled their great Creator-God. This great God, according to the Chinese, made not only man, but the earth and all life in it— as well as the entire universe!

God (ShangTi)

If you look back into the earliest Chinese history, you will find that this Creator-God was called *SHANGTI* 上帝, meaning the *emperor,* 帝 *above* 上. His very name indicates His heavenly rulership. From the most remote time in Chinese history, the sacred BORDER SACRIFICE, described in the previous chapter, was conducted each year for the worship of *ShangTi.* As the emperor himself took part in this annual service dedicated to *ShangTi,* the following words, recorded in the collected statutes of the *Ming* Dynasty (大明會典), were recited which designated *ShangTi* as the CREATOR OF THE WORLD:

帝

emperor

上

above

> Of old in the beginning, there was the great chaos, without form and dark. The five elements [planets] had not begun to re-

volve, nor the sun and moon to shine. You,
O Spiritual Sovereign [神皇] first divided
the grosser parts from the purer. You made
heaven. You made earth. You made man.
All things with their reproducing power
got their being.[1]

ShangTi's continuing regard and love for His created beings are further demonstrated in other recitations from the BORDER SACRIFICE ceremony:

All the numerous tribes of animated beings
are indebted to Thy favour for their
beginnings. Men and things are all empara-
dised in Thy love, O Te. All living things
are indebted to your goodness, but who
knows from whom his blessings come to
him. You alone, O Lord, are the true
parent of all things.[2]

Your sovereign goodness cannot be measured. As a potter You have made all
living things.[3]

He [*ShangTi*] sets fast forever the high
heaven, and establishes the solid earth. His
government is everlasting.[4]

From the foregoing we can learn that *ShangTi* made the heavens and the earth and man. He is the true parent of all things. His love is over all His works. His years are without end. His goodness cannot be measured. This is what the ancient Chinese ancestors believed. Could it be true?

Actually there came to be two BORDER SACRI-

FICES: at the summer solstice a sacrifice to the earth
was observed on the northern border, while the offering to Heaven at the winter solstice on the southern
border gradually became the more important. Said
Confucius in the *Chung-Yung:* "The ceremonies of
the celestial and terrestial sacrifices are those by
which men serve *ShangTi.*"[5]

But even before the reign of the Yellow Emperor, *Huang Ti* (黃帝), in the "legendary period,"
(preceding the first recorded *Hsia* dynasty, 2205-
1766 B.C.), the Chinese were already offering sacrifices to *ShangTi.* For according to the *Historical
Records by Ssu Ma Ch'ien,* we find that they celebrated this rite at Mount Tai in Shan-tung, at the
EASTERN BORDER of China.[6] A BORDER SA-
CRIFICE at an EASTERN locale is still more significant, as we shall subsequently learn.

Did *ShangTi* die along with the imperial reign
in China in 1911? The Chinese today are certainly
not ignorant of *ShangTi,* but few really appreciate
Him as the ORIGINAL GOD OF CHINA, the Creator
of heaven and earth. Is it possible that though
unknown and unappreciated, *ShangTi* is still the
Supreme Ruler, not only of the Chinese, but over
ALL of earth's inhabitants, since He created them
all?

After the sixth century B.C. introduction of

Confucianism and Taoism, followed by Buddhism from India in the first century B.C., *ShangTi* was largely forgotten as the one and only God of the Chinese. However, all traces and knowledge of the original God of China have not been erased. WE BELIEVE THAT A BEAUTIFUL HISTORY OF THE BEGINNINGS OF THE HUMAN RACE ON THE NEWLY CREATED PLANET EARTH HAVE BEEN PERFECTLY PRESERVED IN THE ANCIENT WRITTEN CHARACTERS OF THE CHINESE LANGUAGE! The written language was invented simultaneously with the development of the early Chinese culture.

According to tradition, *Tsieng Chih,* a minister of the same early Yellow Emperor, *Huang Ti,* invented the first characters which have been thought to be simple drawings of familiar objects.[7] Picture words (pictographs) were the earliest form of writing in the ancient world. Other peoples living at the same time in Egypt and Sumeria also had their own pictographic writing. The Chinese inventor of the writing found that by combining two or more pictographs, a story could be related, and thus a new idea expressed. In this way, the ideographic (an idea in writing) character was born. Ideographs, in order to be meaningful, would have to be based upon concepts or knowledge commonly held and understood by these ancient people.

Familiar historical events of a sacred nature, such as the creation of the first man and woman; the original relationship between *ShangTi* and man; how sin began and God's remedy for it; etc., appear to have been the subjects of great interest, and were therefore incorporated into their ideographs, as we shall shortly clearly see.

Once the characters had been invented and accepted, they gradually lost their original historical connections. WITH THE PASSAGE OF CENTURY AFTER CENTURY, THE ORIGIN AND TRUE MEANING OF THESE CHARACTERS WERE LOST AND BECAME MYSTERIOUS, EVEN AS *SHANGTI* ALSO BECAME MYSTERIOUS.

To add to the difficulty in analyzing the characters, scribes through the centuries expressed the ideas of the characters with artistic variations, thus producing many ways of writing a single character. Finally, the great conqueror, *Ch'in Shih Huang Ti,* around 220 B.C., had one of his ministers, *Li Ssu,* standardize the writing with production of the Lesser Seal script.[8]

There have been minor modifications such as the *Li* and *Ts'ao* since, so that today's characters are "shorthand" editions of the early pictographs. For this reason WE WILL EXAMINE THE MOST

ANCIENT CHARACTER FORMS KNOWN, ES-
PECIALLY THE BRONZEWARE AND ORACLE
BONE SCRIPTS, TO LEARN THE ORIGINAL
INTENTION AND MEANINGS. On these artifacts,
the characters are pictographically better depicted
and can be more easily deciphered.

Bronzeware ceremonial vessels, dating back as
far as the *Shang* dynasty (1711-1122 B.C.), have been
beautifully preserved. Many of these contain inscriptions INSIDE the vessels, written, of course, in the
character forms of that day. Characters incised on
bones and tortoise shells, used for divination, hence
called "Oracle Bones," have been another source of
the oldest extant writing.

The first attempt at analyzing the Chinese
characters to learn the true meaning of the ancient
ideographs was attempted by *Hsu Shen* in 86 B.C.,
but his catalog, the *Shuo Wen,* was not published
until about 120 A.D.[9] Most Chinese dictionaries are
still based upon the *Shou Wen.* More recent analyses,
even in English (e.g. Wieger, Wilder and Ingram),
are also largely drawn from the same ancient source.

However, by *Hsu Shen's* day, Taoist ideas had
almost completely replaced the original ancient
religious beliefs in a single Creator-God, *ShangTi.*
Hsu Shen naturally analyzed the characters according
to the current knowledge and thinking of his day.

Since the original intentions of the inventor had long since been buried in the dust of passing ages, how could the true ideas behind many of the ancient characters ever be recovered? Or were they to be forever lost—an unsolvable mystery?

The idea of comparing certain Chinese ideographic characters with another extremely old historical document, the Hebrew sacred writings, has produced startling results. The account of earth's origin in the Hebrew writings and the Chinese concepts of history as recorded in their pictographic and ideographic characters are identical! ONE OF THE PURPOSES OF THIS BOOK IS TO BRING TOGETHER AND DEMONSTRATE THE SIMI-LARITY OF THE HISTORICAL NARRATIVES OF THE TWO WIDELY SEPARATED CHINESE AND HEBREW ANCIENT CIVILIZATIONS.

In the epilog, we will comment briefly on the two methods of analysis: the *Shuo Wen* and our "hieroglyphic" system—"hiero" indicating "sacred", and "glyph" meaning "engraving." Were the Chinese pictograms and ideograms drawn from objects and activities of everyday life, or were they more specifically oriented to the ancients' knowledge of sacred history? By the end of the book, you will be better able to judge the merits of the "hieroglyphic" system here introduced.

The oldest of the Hebrew narratives was written about 1500 B.C., at least seven centuries AFTER the Chinese writing came into being. From earliest human memory and tradition, as well as through inspiration from the God of the Hebrews, a prophet, Moses, recorded the beginnings of earth's history. The first book of the Hebrew scriptures is called Genesis—"Beginnings."

It is indeed interesting to examine the recitation of the Chinese BORDER SACRIFICE rites worshiping *ShangTi,* with reference to the first verses of the Hebrew Genesis, which also names the Creator-God. Read again the recitation given at the beginning of the chapter and note the similarity with excerpts from the more detailed story as recorded in the Hebrew writings:

> In the beginning God created the heaven and the earth. And the earth was without form, and void; and darkness was upon the face of the deep. . . .
>
> And God said, "Let the waters under the heavens be gathered together into one place, and let the dry land appear." And it was so. God called the dry land Earth, and the waters that were gathered together he called Seas. . . .
>
> And God made the two great lights, the greater light to rule the day, and the lesser light to rule the night, he made the stars also. . . .

> So God created man in his own image, . . .
> male and female he created them. And God
> blessed them, and God said to them, "Be
> fruitful and multiply, and fill the earth and
> subdue it; and have dominion over the fish
> of the sea and over the birds of the air and
> over every living thing that moves upon
> the earth."[10]

ShangTi surely appears to be one and the same as the God of the Hebrews. In fact, one of the Hebrew names for their God was *El SHADDAI*, phonetically very similar to *SHANGTI*, especially in the Cantonese dialect which pronounces the name *"SHANGDAI"*. Cantonese, incidentally, is thought to be closest to the original spoken Chinese.

Let us now begin an investigation of earth's primal history by analyzing some old and simple Chinese characters. At the same time, we will compare stories contained in them with the ancient Hebrew narratives.

CHAPTER 3

CHINESE CONCEPTS OF EARTH'S BEGINNINGS

The ancient mystery regarding the origin and identity of *ShangTi* 上帝 has been solved. As we have learned, the "BORDER SACRIFICE" to *ShangTi* clearly identifies Him as the Creator-God of the universe. The next question is HOW did *ShangTi* create all things? Note one further recitation from this ancient rite:

> When *Te* [*ShangTi*], the Lord, had so decreed, He CALLED INTO EXISTENCE heaven, earth, and man. Between heaven and earth He separately placed in order men and things, all overspread by the heavens.[1]

Notice that *ShangTi,* according to the ancient Chinese record, "CALLED INTO EXISTENCE

19

heaven, earth and man.'' Compare this with the way the Hebrew text describes the method of creation by their God, *El SHADDAI,* (whom we suspect is identical with *ShangTi,* as the similarity in name and role would suggest):

> The Lord created the heavens by his command, the sun, moon and stars by his spoken word . . . WHEN HE SPOKE, THE WORLD WAS CREATED; at his command everything appeared.[2]

The Chinese and Hebrew records are identical. *ShangTi* simply spoke objects into being as His vast energy, expressed as a command, was transformed into matter, or visible created objects. He thus probably followed an elementary law of nature: MASS AND ENERGY CAN NEITHER BE CREATED NOR DESTROYED, BUT ENERGY CAN BE CONVERTED INTO MASS, OR MASS INTO ENERGY. Plants and animals sprang into being at His command! But most wonderful of all, His whole creative work of producing not only our earth, but also the whole planetary system out of nothing, took but six ordinary twenty-four hour days. The lovely new earth in perfect order emerged from chaotic darkness.

A summary of the Hebrew record[3] reveals that on the first day He created light and drove out the darkness which covered the deep rolling waters on the earth's surface. The second day He divided the waters surrounding the earth and in this space created the atmospheric heavens with its life-supporting gases. The third day *ShangTi* pushed back the waters over portions of the earth and formed seas. Upon the dry land which appeared, He BROUGHT FORTH vegetation with plants yielding seed to reproduce themselves. At the close of each day He saw that everything was very good.

The fourth day, *ShangTi* made the sun, moon, and planets, and set them in motion around the earth to produce the days, months, and seasons. On the fifth day He brought forth swarms of living creatures in the seas, and birds in the skies. All creatures were given reproductive powers.

The sixth day, *ShangTi* said, "Let the earth BRING FORTH living creatures according to their kinds . . . And it was so."[4]

Here *ShangTi* COMMANDS the EARTH to BRING FORTH living animals. A Bronzeware form of the radical, *to produce, bring forth life* 生 (B)[5] (生), shows God Ψ with arms upraised (we will confirm this symbol Ψ as "God" more conclusively later), and the *earth* 土 (B)[6] (土). Furthermore, the character, *to speak, to tell* in the Bronzeware form 告 (B)[7] (告), combines *to bring forth* 生 with a

bring forth life

earth, dust

mouth

to tell, speak

mouth ∀ (B) (⊡). Contained within this one character ∀̌ we find all the elements of creation: GOD ψ BRINGS FORTH ψ̱ life from the EARTH ⊥ by SPEAKING ∀̌ with His MOUTH ∀ .

At the outset, we should explain our format used throughout the book. It may initially appear rather complicated, but actually is quite simple. A subscript in parenthesis following a character indicates the source of the ancient form: B (Bronzeware); O (Oracle Bone); S (Seal); U (Unidentified source; a hybrid; artistic variation). Use of one of these markers will circumvent having to repeat information regarding origin of the character in the text.

Since adding "heads" to the ancient Chinese stick figures makes them "come alive" and easier to visualize, this depiction will follow in parenthesis where appropriate. When character discussions are more detailed, a system of summarizing formulae will serve to clarify the analysis, e.g.:

$$ψ\,(\overset{\circ}{ψ})_+ \quad \underline{⌊} \quad = \quad \underline{ψ} \quad + \quad ∀ \quad = \quad ∀̌$$

God	dust	to bring forth	mouth	to speak, tell

The foregoing is a simple illustration for the non-Chinese readership, demonstrating how an ideographic character is cleverly formed. The "ABC's" of the Chinese writing are the most primitive symbols, and often little pictographs which are called "radicals." There are 214 of them, e.g.: ⊥ (土); ⊌ (口). Radicals may be combined to form more complex radicals, as 坐 (生); or with addition of other radical(s), a character, as 告 (告). IN OUR FORMAT, SINCE THE ANCIENT FORMS ARE MORE PICTOGRAPHIC, THEY WILL BE USED AND WILL APPEAR BEFORE TODAY'S RENDITIONS IN PARENTHESIS, e.g.: 告 (告).

The creation of mankind also took place on the sixth day, but was more special than that of all the other creatures. The actual creation of the first man is pictured in a second name for God, *Shen* 示 (S)[8] (神). In this character, the left radical 示 is a "God" radical (this will also be explained later); but the right radical, pictures two *hands* reaching down from above. Hands reaching from above such as ⟨ or ⟩ , we will learn, are usually God's hands. (Later we will find the hands reaching upward ΨΨ would appear to be man's hands.) But what do we find in *Shen's* hands? The most primitive drawing of a *person* is | .

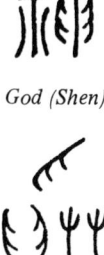

God (Shen)

hands

示	+	⟨⟩	+	︱ (?)	=	示
God radical		hands		person		God (Shen)

This radical (申), incidentally, by itself

meaning *to instruct, to explain,* is even more clearly written in a Bronzeware inscription as ⊕ (B).[9] Remember that we are looking at very simple pictures. To make sure that we understand that | is a *person* a large dot ● has been added, as ♦. A large dot shaped as ● (B)[10], ♥ (B)[11], or ■ (B)[12], (T) indicated an *adult male!*

to instruct

adult male

$$ () \quad + \quad | \, (\, ? \,) + \quad ● \quad = \quad ⊕ $$

hands   person   adult male   to instruct

The first human being on earth, according to not only the Chinese, but also the Hebrew record, was a fully grown ADULT MAN who came forth from the HANDS of God (*Shen*). In the Hebrew scriptures, this is the record of man's creation:

> And the Lord God formed man from the DUST OF THE EARTH and breathed in his nostrils the breath of life, and man became a living soul.[13]

We learn that this man's name was "Adam." In the Hebrew, this means *ground* and also *red.* Note how the Chinese writing once more agrees with these designations. The radical, *soil, earth* ⊥ (B)(土), as etched inside ancient bronzeware vessels, shows a *person* | , an *adult male* ● , coming up from the ground _ beneath him.

丨 (𠂉) +	●	+	—	=	⼟
person	*adult male*		*ground*		*earth, dust*

Another representation of the creation of Adam is found in the radical, *body* �(† (B)[14] (身). This radical is phonetically similar to *Shen*. Adam's was the first *body* formed on the new earth. 亻 (B)[15] (人) represents a *person or Being*. In this instance, 亻 represents the Creator who is bending over an object. (It may be more clearly perceived if we draw a head on the pictogram: 亻 . One Oracle Bone form, 𠂤 [16], also shows the Creator's *hand* ⼂ more distinctly.) Adam is this time depicted as ☉ , and note that he is being formed from the earth beneath — . But if you are acquainted with ancient Chinese, you might be thinking that ☉ (B) means *sun* (日). You are also correct, and therefore ☉ means *dawn or early morning*, as well. Here we see a clever double meaning: Adam must have been created in the early morning on the sixth day.

In the Bronzeware writing, the character *dawn* ☉ (B)[17] (旦), contained an *adult male* ● (丁), covered by the *sun* ☉ . What can this mean? Why should Adam be represented as a sun, or covered by the sun? Actually, we see a pictogram of a *person, mouth* ○ (B)[18] (口). (Recall the common idiom in designating *persons:* so many *mouths* to feed?) The

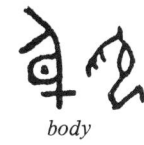

body

person, Being

dawn

sun

person, mouth

small dot • in the center represents a *flame of fire*.

flame of fire

$$\bigcirc \quad + \quad \cdot \quad = \quad \odot \quad + \quad \bullet \quad = \quad \raisebox{-2pt}{\large ♀}$$

mouth, person	flame of fire	sun	adult male	dawn

Adam had a fiery appearance, as the brightness of the *sun,* for we learn from the Hebrew Genesis:

> Then God said, "And now we will make human beings; they will BE LIKE US and RESEMBLE us."[19]

What does *ShangTi* (*Shen*) look like? The Hebrew scriptures again inform us:

"The Lord God is a SUN and shield."[20] It also says: "Our God is a consuming FIRE."[21] God's glory is as a fire or as the sun, and Adam was made to "look like" or "resemble" his Creator.

fire

A Bronzeware inscription for *fire* is $\overset{.}{\perp}$ (B)[22] (火). This would also support the idea that the first *adult male* ●, who was formed from the *dust* $\perp$ of the earth, had the appearance of *fire* $\overset{.}{\perp}$, as well as the *sun* ⊙ .

$$| \; (\raisebox{-2pt}{♀}) + \quad \bullet \quad + \quad \_ \quad = \quad \overset{.}{\perp} \quad + \quad \cdot\cdot \quad = \quad \overset{.}{\perp}$$

person	adult male	ground	dust	flames	fire

To be created resembling God meant that Adam

was PERFECT and SINLESS, even as *ShangTi* (*Shen*) is perfect. *ShangTi's* dazzling perfection is spoken of as His "glory" which is represented as a fiery or sunlike appearance. Therefore, Adam, the first man, was originally clothed in a glorious shining light, even as God.

Again, we read from the Hebrew sacred writings:

> O Lord, my God, how great you are! You are CLOTHED with majesty and GLORY; YOU COVER YOURSELF WITH LIGHT.[23]

to be like, resemble

The character *to be like* ⽣ (B)[24] (若) must surely refer to the very fact of Adam's *likeness* to God. In ⽣ we recognize not one God, ⼼ with arms upraised, but three ⽣ acting together as one! How can this be?

Review again the Hebrew text:

> Then God [*Elohim*] said: "And now WE will make human beings: they will *be like* US and *resemble* US."[25]

Here, the name, *Elohim,* used for "God" is a plural noun. Note also the plural pronouns "we" and "us." As we proceed, we will find that both the Chinese and Hebrews had the same concept of God—three Personalities working as One, called the TRINITY. We will shortly find other examples of this.

Cheng Hsuan, a scholar of the early *Han* dynasty, stated: "Heaven is another name for *ShangTi.*"[26]

*God, Heaven
(T'ien)*

*noble person,
great*

So the Chinese have a third name (besides *ShangTi* 上帝 and *Shen* 神 for God—*T'ien, Heaven* (B)[27] (天). As we have studied the Bronzeware characters, it appears that a "blackening" of a symbol also indicates "glory." We find this in the character for *Heaven* , where the "head" is blackened. 大(B) (大), by itself represents a *great, noble person.* So God, *Heaven* , in the Chinese thinking, was represented as a "noble Being" clothed with "majesty and glory." This would also explain why God's fingers are "blackened" in ⑶ (p. 24) as well as why the depiction of God's *hand(s)* ⑶ , ⑵ , ⑶ , always show just three fingers—representing the TRINITY at work.

We can understand, too, why Adam, the first *adult male* ●, created in the image of *God, Heaven* (天), was also portrayed as a "glorious" *person*

In summary, we thus learn that, before Adam sinned and disobeyed God, his body was covered with a glorious light, giving him a fiery appearance.

The Hebrew text comments:

The man and his wife were both naked, and they felt no shame.[28]

naked, red

Adam, and later his wife, were unashamed to appear before *ShangTi* naked—why? The Chinese character *naked, red* 赤(B)[29] (赤) shows a *noble* 大(B)(大) man and a *fire* 火. Adam and his wife were made in the image of God. Adam's body at this time was naked except for a glorious fiery covering—possibly also red-tinged! Earlier in this chapter it was mentioned that in Hebrew the name "Adam," means not only "ground," but also "red." It must have been Adam's fiery covering which made both the Chinese and Hebrews describe him as being "red."

> You made him [man] a little lower than God and crowned him with GLORY and honor.[30]

大 (夫)	+	火	=	炙
noble (man)		*fire*		*naked*

intelligent, civilized

This same fiery appearance is also seen in the significant character, *intelligent, civilized* 夈 (B)[31] (文) which confirms and records Adam's *refinement*. Earth's first man, 夫 , is here decorated with a glorious *flame* • , indicating again his likeness to God!

Analysis of ancient Chinese characters reveals that our world's first man had been formed perfect, sinless, and noble in body and character. His origin was from *ShangTi*, Himself, and not from a spontaneous evolutionary process which would eliminate *ShangTi* as Creator.

It is likely that the original pictograph for

Father

Father 𠬝 (B)[32] (父) refers to God, the heavenly Parent. Note the "blackening" (glory) of this "etherial-appearing" Person with uplifted arms, characteristic of God. Review once more the BORDER SACRIFICE recitation:

> All the numerous tribes of animated beings are indebted to Thy favour for their beginning. Men and things are all emparadised in Thy love, O Te. All living things are indebted to your goodness, but who knows from whom his blessings come to him. You alone, O Lord, are the TRUE PARENT of all things.[33]

Frequently encountered on the Bronzeware is this association, 𠬝 (B),[34] once more suggesting the heavenly *Father* 𠬝 "forming" Adam, the first *adult male* ●

vessel

A specific detail of Adam's creation is found in the character, *vessel* (B)[35] (卣). This time the *Being* ◯ (God) is enfolding the "*dust*man," 土 (B) (土), Adam. But why is Adam called a "*vessel?*" Recall that *ShangTi* was referred to as a POTTER in the BORDER SACRIFICE recitation:

> Your sovereign goodness cannot be measured. As a POTTER You have made all living things.[36]

Compare this Chinese concept with the Hebrew scripture:

> Yet, O Lord, You are our FATHER. We
> are the CLAY, You are the POTTER; we
> are all the work of your hand.[37]

How fitting that Adam should be called a
"vessel," for he had been sculpted from clay, the dust
of the ground! We concluded previously that he had
been formed at dawn on the sixth day of earth's first
week (p. 25), for all during that day he was given the
intriguing task of naming the animals as the great
POTTER formed them:

good

> So God took some soil from the ground
> and formed all the animals and all the
> birds. Then He brought them to the man to
> see what he would name them: and that is
> how they all got their names. So the man
> named all the birds and all the animals;
> but NOT ONE OF THEM WAS A SUIT-
> ABLE COMPANION TO HELP HIM.[38]

woman

It was not *ShangTi's* intention to leave Adam
without a mate. So as this first momentous sixth
day was drawing to a close, we read again from the
Hebrew writings:

man,
offspring

> Then the Lord God said, "It is not GOOD
> for the man to live alone . . . "[39]

What God implied was that it was *good*  (B)[40]
(好) for a *man*  to have a *woman*  for a mate.

| woman | + | man | = | good |

31

Was Adam's mate to be made of the soil as he had been? No, this was not God's beautiful and meaningful purpose. Adam would appreciate his wife even more when he learned *ShangTi's* unique plan for the creation of woman!

CHAPTER 4

THE RIB STORY

As the sixth glorious day of creation was drawing to a close and the sun was beginning to sink toward the western horizon, Adam expressed his wonder that God had not provided a companion for him. Each of the animals, which he had just spent the day naming, had a mate by its side.

Recall the character ⟳ (B) (𦣻), *vessel*, illustrating Adam's creation (p. 30). Another ancient artistic depiction of this symbol is ⟳ (B)[1]. Showing the glorious *flame of fire* • , (p. 26). Let us now examine a similar "flask-like" figure portraying God, a *Being* ⟳, this time enclosing *two* ⩠ *persons* / , the radical *west* ⟳ (B)[2] (西).

vessel

west

$$\triangle\ (\overset{\circ}{\triangle})\ +\ \diagdown\diagdown\ +\ /\ (\ \int\ )\ =\ \text{⟳}$$

| God (a Being) | two | person(s) | west |

33

The Rib Story

It was evidently as the sun was setting in the *west* that God brought forth the second person. The details of God's plan are most interesting. We learn from the Hebrew record that God said:

> "I will make a suitable companion to help him." . . . Then the Lord God made the man fall into a deep sleep, and while he was sleeping, he took out one of the man's ribs and closed up the flesh. He formed a woman out of the rib and brought her to him.[3]

dusk, to marry

A second character which confirms the time and method of creating Adam's mate is 🜨 (O)[4] (昏), meaning both *dusk* and *to marry*. In 🜨 we find the great *Being* (God) bending over the *glorified person* (▣), Adam. Having these two widely diverging meanings—*dusk* and *to marry*—it can only be interpreted as God ( ) performing the first operation in which he removes a rib from the sleeping Adam (▣ , p. 25), and from it forms a beautiful wife for him. Again it emphasizes the time of day, *dusk,* when Adam's mate was created and the first *marriage* performed by God, Himself.

flesh

We can even see this very operation in today's radical form *flesh* 肉 , where 冂 is *entered* 入 to take out a *person* 人. But it is even more clear in the ancient form from which today's radical was possibly transcribed, (U)[5] (肉). Here, (人) represents a *man,* Adam, while we find ✗ (子) attached to him, meaning not only a *man, son, offspring,* but also a *bride* or *wife*! Note God's *hand* ⟡ reaching inside the *man* ⟡ to bring out the *wife* ✗. And what did Adam exclaim upon awakening?

wife, son, offspring

> At last, here is one of my own kind—bone taken from my bone, and FLESH from my FLESH. Woman is her name because she was taken out of man.[6]

man, Being

⟡ (⟡) +	⟡	+	✗	=	⟡
person	*hand (God's)*		*wife*		*flesh*

Surely the ancient Chinese as well as the Hebrews knew as fact the earliest history of the world and the creation of man and woman!

SINCE MAN WAS CREATED TO RESEMBLE GOD WE WOULD EXPECT THAT HE BE SIMILAR IN APPEARANCE. HENCE THE CHINESE PICTOGRAM FOR MAN ⟡ (AS IN ⟡) RESEMBLES THE DEPICTION OF GOD AS A BEING ⟡ , (AS IN ⟡ AND ⟡). THIS SIMILARITY SHOULD BE BORNE IN MIND AS WE PROCEED TO ANALYZE CHARACTERS.

What joy Adam knew, especially when he realized that Eve, as he now named his companion, was actually a part of him! God also must have

enjoy

enjoyed (B)[7](享) seeing the first pair so happy with each other. (白) meaning a *vessel*, is an apt description of Adam, formed from clay by the heavenly Potter. From the *vessel*, we find a second *person* 0 (口) emerging—depicting the origin of Eve in Adam.

$$△ (△) + \cdot = △ + O = ♀$$

| God | flame of glory | vessel (Adam) | person (Eve) | enjoy |

sufficient, announce

God knew that just two persons were *sufficient* (B)[8] (身), for he *announced* to them,

"Be fruitful and multiply, and fill the earth and subdue it; and have dominion . . . over every living thing that moves upon the earth."[9]

In , we find the TRINITY again, the three Persons of the Godhead who took part in creation (see ,
p. 27), with uplifted arms: . Compare this character also with the preceding one,).

a second

We have already noted the heavenly *Father* hovering over the first *adult male* ● , Adam (p. 30). We find the Father also pictured on the Bronzeware (B)[10], equally interested in a *second* (B)[11](乙) person, Eve. Another inscription, (B)[11] appears to locate the site of Adam's creation: a holy *mountain* (B)[12](山). (Note the

36

"blackening" of this symbol, which we believe indicates "holy").

To verify even more solidly the assumed site of Adam and Eve's creation, let us examine the character *to create,*  ₍ᵦ₎[13] (造). In it we find the *mountain* and recognize *to bring forth* ⊻ and *to speak* from a previous discussion (p. 22). The 身 ₍ᵦ₎ (舟) needs analysis. Although 身 is a *vessel,* it is NOT a boat in this instance. We have just learned that Adam was called a *vessel* ⚲, because he had been formed from clay by the Creator. Eve, in turn, had been formed from Adam's rib. Both were, in truth, "vessels." A close examination of 身 in a slightly different artistic rendition,  ₍ᵦ₎[14] shows two joined, back-to-back, bowing persons: 刁 + 𝚪 .

mountain

to create

vessel

$$\Psi + \mathbf{\bot} = \underline{\Psi} + \sigma = \overset{\curlyvee}{\circ} + \amalg + \sqcap = \text{创}$$

God (Potter) — clay — bring forth — mouth — speak — vessel(s) — moun-tain — create

to be, exist, possess

We find this same radical 身 ₍ᵦ₎ (舟) in  ₍ᵦ₎[15] (有), *to be, exist.* From the *Father's* ⇃ ₍ᵦ₎[16] (父) hand again we find the first pair come into *existence.* Here the *Father* ⇃ is depicted a bit more cursive, as is 𝔧 , which is sometimes transcribed as *flesh*  ₍ᵤ₎[17] (肉). The first humans were actually God's *possession*  , another meaning of this character.

Father

flesh

God (Shen)

So close was the relationship between the Creator and the first couple, that we find them an integral part of *Shen's* 〔U〕[18] (神) name, in many different ways of writing it. In this rendition, we find Adam and Eve once more portrayed as *suns* , or "glorified persons," while God is the great *Being* leaning over them.

$$ \text{⊓} \quad + \quad \text{Being} \quad ( ) \quad + \quad = \quad + \quad \text{○} \quad = \quad \text{〔God (Shen)〕} $$

God radical	Being	two	suns	God (Shen)

In yet another artistic variation of *Shen,* 〔U〕[18] (神), we see that couple conjoined. This appears to be a modification of a Bronzeware depiction, *to instruct* 〔B〕[19] (申). The very fact that there are not TWO *"suns"* , , supports our interpretation that the *suns* ○ represent the glorified Adam and Eve. Furthermore, the inscription, , depicts two *mouths, persons* ⊔ (口)!

to instruct

filial,
honor parent

The bond between God and the first couple is portrayed also in *filial, to honor one's parents* 〔B〕[20] (孝). God is found with upraised arms 火 , and the clever ancient Chinese melded this symbol with the *Father* 〔 父 〕. We have interpreted 〈 , formed in the configuration, as a *mountain*, while 〔 子 〕 is a *person, offspring.*

火 (灾) +　　ㄨ　　+　　𝔂　　=　　𩐇

God　　　　　Father　　　offspring　　　filial

Another rendition of *filial* 𩐇 (B)[21] varies slightly, but carries EXACTLY the same meaning. God, this time, is replaced by "⁄ , three strokes, which are seen repeatedly in Chinese Script. We believe the symbol "⁄ represents "God's presence," the TRINITY, the three Persons of the Godhead. In the pictogram 𩐇 , we find there are *two* ·· *persons* 𝔂 , BOTH Adam and Eve.

"⁄　+　ㄨ　+　` ´　+　𝔂　=　𩐇

God's　　Father　　two　　persons　　filial
presence

We are thus given the idea of God as a Parent and 𝔂 as two *offspring*. We may also understand why in *flesh* ⊛ , the *wife* 𝔂 , Eve, was as an "offspring" of Adam, formed from his very body!

What was the home which God prepared for Adam and Eve like? According to the ancient Chinese, it was a *palace* 宫 (B)[22] , 宫 (O)[23] (宫). Under the *roof* ⌂ , are two *persons* ▽ + ▽ and □ + □ cleverly united, ▽ and 田 . *ShangTi* conducted the first marriage ceremony, as the Hebrew text describes it:

palace

Therefore a man . . . is united with his wife and they will become ONE FLESH.[24]

roof

An alternate pictogram of *palace* 館 (U)[25] shows this exactly, where under one *roof* 𠆢 (宀), the couple 呂 (呂) are united as ONE *FLESH* 𠕎 (肉).

a couple

呂	+	𠕎	+	𠆢	=	館
couple		*flesh*		*roof*		*palace*

ShangTi completed 十 (B)[26] (十) creating the earth in but SIX twenty-four hour DAYS. This radical, *complete, perfect* 十 , clearly shows the finishing of God's work. The last creative act was to *bring forth* 𡉚 the first *adult male* ● from the *dust of the ground* 土. He was *perfect* 十 and holy. Eve, in turn, was formed from Adam later on this sixth day. The creation of these first two humans *completed* the earth and its furnishings. We read from the Hebrew writings:

complete

Thus the heavens and the earth were COMPLETED in all their vast array. By the seventh day God had finished the work he had been doing; so on the SEVENTH day he RESTED from all his work. And God BLESSED the seventh day and made it holy, because on it he rested from all the work of creating that he had done.[27]

One can see that the ancient Chinese, as well as

40

the Hebrews, understood that the *seventh* day was blessed, for the older symbol ╪ (B,O)[28] (七), *seven,* shows the familiar pose of God with arms outstretch-ed (夲). Another rendition, ㇄ (U)[29] (七) for *seven* portrays God even more unmistakably, sitting with arm upraised in BLESSING (㇄).

seven

The word, *to rest, stop* 止 (B),[30] 止 (O)[30] (止), likewise has significance in the original writing. This radical is used in many characters, as we shall soon discover. 止 and 止 are simple pictographs of a foot. From the "blackening" of 止 , we can gather that it represents *ShangTi's* foot, *stopped* or *resting* from His six days' work of creating the earth and its contents. Note that the character, *blessing* 祉 (O)[31] (祉), for example, contains the God radical 丅 (p. 23) and *to rest, stop* 止 (止), making it clear that 止 is God's foot.

to rest, stop

blessing

丅	+	止	=	祉
God radical		*to rest*		*BLESSING*

Thus the weekly cycle of seven days was es-tablished at creation, and has been kept ever since, worldwide, as the *returning seventh day* 七日來復 (a Chinese saying). The week is not regulated by the movement of the earth, sun, moon, or stars, but reflects ONLY the great historic work of the Creator,

ShangTi. He gave this day of rest to Adam and Eve and their descendants so that men everywhere might weekly remember His great creative acts.

CHAPTER 5

SECRETS OF
A LOST GARDEN

From the Chinese writing we learn that in the *beginning* 丂 (B)[1] (元), there were just *two* 二 *persons* 勹 on earth. Futhermore, another Bronzeware rendition of *beginning* 丂 (B)[2] reveals that the original couple had sinless characters. They were reflectors of *God, Heaven* 夨 (B) (天), for Adam, the first *adult male* ● (丁), was designated as a holy *person* O by the "blackening" of this symbol (p. 28).

丂 丂

beginning

二   +   勹 (勹) +   ●   =   丂

two   *persons*   *adult male*   *beginning*
                                  ("glorious")

The man was named Adam, meaning "the ground," from which he had been created by God. In

Ω Δ

ground, dust

addition to ±̇ (B) (土) meaning *ground, dust* we may also examine two inscriptions from Oracle Bones for *ground* Ω (O)[3] and Δ (O)[4]. These further confirm Adam as a *person (mouth)* O , Δ arising from the ground — beneath (see 𝑎̣ , p. 24). And we learn that "Adam called his wife's name Eve, because she was the mother of all living."[5]

TⒶ Δ

ancestor,
founder,
prototype,
original

Thus we find the record of the first two *ancestors* TⒶ (O), Δ (O)[6] (祖). Comparing Ω and Δ above, representing Adam arising from the earth, we find not only Adam, but *two* ⹀ persons, he and also his wife, Eve, "the mother of all living." The *ancestors* TⒶ are found with the God radical T , indicating that *ShangTi* is, of course, the ultimate ancestor in whose image Adam and Eve had been created. This character denotes not only *ancestor,* but also the *founder, prototype, original, beginning!*

$$ T \;+\; = \;+\; O \;+\; - \;=\; T\!Ⓐ $$

| God radical | two | persons (mouth) | ground | ancestor |

𝄇

family, race

We find, then, that Adam was the founder of the whole human *family, race* 𝄇 (B)[7] (族). This *noble* 𝄐 (大), holy *adult man* ● had been created by God Ψ on the holy mountain ⊓ .

Ψ + ⊓ = 𝕩 + 大 + • = 𝕩

| God | mountain | central, place | noble | adult man | family, race |

family

A second character meaning *family* 𝕩 (B)[8] (氏), again shows a *perfect* ⵏ *adult male* • *person* 𝕩 (𝕩) as the founder of the whole human *family* (compare also 𝕩 , p. 43).

Just what kind of an environment did *ShangTi* provide for our first parents? From the Hebrew scripture, we read a description:

> And the Lord God planted a Garden in Eden, in the east; and there he put the man whom he had formed. And out of the ground the Lord God made to grow every tree that is pleasant to the sight and good for food, the Tree of Life also in the midst of the Garden, and the Tree of the Knowledge of Good and Evil. A river flowed out of Eden to water the Garden, and there it divided and became four rivers.[9]

This garden paradise has actually been illustrated with drawings in the Chinese calligraphy. A much used radical, *garden, landed property* ⊞ (B)[10],

*garden, field
landed property*

⊞ (U)[11] (田), would seem to specifically have reference to this first lovely Garden of Eden. At first glance, it appears to be a well-irrigated *field*, but the Bronzeware inscription, depicted as ⊞, presents a different idea, especially in the light of the Hebrew

45

description that there was a river flowing out of Eden to water the Garden which divided into four rivers. According to this pictograph, the river originated in the very center, with streams flowing in four directions ⊹.

The second ancient form here presented, 🔲, gives additional insight, revealing the wellspring of the four-headed river, as we shall discover in the next paragraph.

fountain

Immediately we wonder what the source of the river might be. Most rivers originate from converging streams high in the mountains. Let us examine an earlier form of *spring* or *fountain* 𝔐 (B)[12] (泉) which appears to be an accurate portrayal of a fountain gushing upward and bears resemblance to the aforementioned 🔲 figure of *garden*. But note the T (O)[13] (示) inscribed on it. This is an ancient symbol for God!

God

A character phonetically similar to *beginning* 元 *(yüan)*, pictures our first parents, and is a second pictograph of their Eden home, *garden* 圂 (U)[14] (園), also *yüan*. The closeness in sound of these pairs of characters seems more than mere coincidence.

garden

Let us examine this most commonly used character for *Garden* 圂. We find God 屮 with upraised arms (compare 坐 p. 21; 㞢 p. 27; 㞢 p. 36; 㖒 p. 37; and 㿟 p. 38). By now it has become more convincing that this figure **Ψ** represents God. Here He is found on the summit of a *mountain* ∧ . Below is a *mouth* ▢ representing communion: speaking and eating with God. Beneath these are two *people* ⋏ , the second emerging from the side of the first, even as Eve was created from Adam's rib (p. 35). The Garden is *enclosed* ▢ by a boundary.

enclosure

(⚚)

Ψ + ∧ + ▢ + ⋏ + ▢ = 園

God   mountain   mouth   two   enclosure   garden
persons

Listen to what the Hebrew text tells us about God's mountain, the river, the fountain and the couple:

> Your righteousness is like the MOUN-
> TAINS OF GOD. . .
> How precious is Your lovingkindness, O
> God!
> Therefore the CHILDREN OF MEN put
> their trust under the shadow of Your
> wings.
> They are abundantly satisfied with the
> fullness of Your HOUSE
> And You give them drink from the RIVER
> of Your pleasures
> For with You is the FOUNTAIN OF
> LIFE.[15]

Again, both the Chinese characters and the Hebrew scripture appear to portray several identical features of the first Garden home:

47

1. A four-headed river flows from the *Garden* ⊞ and waters it.

2. The source of the river is a *fountain* 𝕸 in the center.

3. The *Fountain* 𝕸 is also symbolic of *God* 丅, Himself, as the "Fountain of Life."

4. The *Garden* 🅰 encompasses "God's *mountain*" ∧, His "house," or dwelling place.

5. Two *people* 🆇, "the children of men," come to commune there with God. (This includes "feasting"—apparently on fruit from the Tree of Life—and drinking from the River of Life. Eating and drinking from these two sources assured Adam and Eve of immortality.)

Recall that two specific trees, the Tree of Life and the Tree of the Knowledge of Good and Evil, were mentioned previously in the Eden description:

> In the MIDDLE of the Garden were the Tree of Life and the Tree of the Knowledge of Good and Evil.[16]

These two important trees therefore must have been located on the mountain in the center of the Garden as well. We have already specified that the Fountain was symbolic of God and was the source of the four-headed River of Life which originated from the CENTER of the Garden.

central, place 丂

The radical meaning *center, place* 丂 (U)[17] (方)

itself, provides the same information. The earlier writing 㐌 , is actually a pictogram of *ShangTi* as a great *Being, Person* 㐌 , AGAIN WITH ARMS UPRAISED 㐌 . Compare also the Bronzeware rendering of *Father* 㣇 (B)[18] (父). We can thus surmise how 十 became an early symbol for God.

Father

It was to this central place in the Garden that Adam and Eve *traveled* 㫃 (B)[19] (旅). How clever that the ancient Chinese calligrapher simply stretched out the radical *central* 㐌 , and formed God on the holy mountain 㝵 . The two *persons* 仢 are easily recognized.

to travel

$$\Psi\ (\Phi) + \sqcap\ =\ \text{㝵}\quad + \text{仢}\ (\text{仢})\ =\ \text{㫃}$$

| God | mountain | central | two persons | to travel |

Another character also meaning *to travel* 㭭 (B)[20] (桓), agrees with our interpretation that a *sun* ☉ (日) frequently depicts a glorified • *person* ○ (口), in this case, a human *couple* 呂 (呂, pp. 25, 38). Here the *couple* 呂 are found at the *Tree* 木 of Life (p. 45) to which they *traveled* to partake of the fruit giving immortality.

to travel

They *returned* 㫌 (O)[21] (旋) there frequently. Again we find their destination is God on the mount 㝵 . They *rested* 止 (O) (止) and communed (spoke and ate with God) there, as specified by the *mouth* ○ .

to return

to rest

God | *mount* | *central* | *rest* | *mouth (communion)* | *to return*

to stop, rest

tree

in front of, before

A second character for *stop, rest* (B)[22] (休) shows a *person* (Adam or Eve) at a *tree* (B) (木). As the Hebrew text stated, the two special trees were located in the MIDDLE of the Garden, so must also have been located on the holy mountain.

It was their privilege to come *before, in front of* (B)[23] (前) God. By now we can readily find God on the mount, and we can also recognize the first couple as "*vessels*" (p. 37).

God | *mount* | *vessel (two people)* | *in front of, before*

quiet, respectful

river, water

They were *quiet, respectful* (B)[24] (兪) as they worshiped Him in this sacred place. We can see the mountain, and this time the river as it flows from God, Himself. Once more the first parents are pictured, bowing in His presence.

mountain | *river* | *vessel (two persons)* | *quiet, respectful*

We can know that this was a holy *place* (B)[25]

(所), for we find "God's presence" ≡ (note the three strokes above the mount ⌐ from which the River of Life *flows* ∥).

place

$$\text{⌐} \quad + \quad \text{≡} \quad + \quad \text{∥} \quad = \quad \overline{\overline{\text{⌐}∥}}$$

mount   "God's presence"   river   place

We can erase the last doubt that the Garden of Eden had a holy *hill* 𡵲 (O)[26], 陵 (B)[27] (陵) when we examine this character. The *mount* 阝, 阝 (B)(阝) is identified by three *mouths* 吕 (the TRINITY), or God's presence ≡ . In 𡵲 we find the *couple* 𠂆 (𠂆); while in 陵 only Adam as the "dustman" 土 appears before *God* 大 the *Father* 𠂆.

(𡗗) (𠂆)

$$\text{≡} \quad + \quad | \quad = \quad \text{阝} \quad + \quad \text{土} \quad + \quad \text{大} \quad + \quad \text{𠂆} \quad = \quad \text{陵}$$

God's (incline) mount "dustman" God Father Hill
presence

Let us make one more relevant comparison with the Hebrew record which reads:

> Who shall ascend the HILL OF THE LORD?
>   And who shall stand in HIS HOLY
>   PLACE?
> He who has clean hands and a pure heart
>   And who does not lift up his soul to
>   what is false and does not swear deceit-
>   fully,
> He will receive BLESSING from the
>   Lord . . .[28]

It surely seems that the Hebrew scripture and the Chinese ideographs are describing the same place and activity! Adam and Eve could *travel* to the *HILL* OF THE LORD and stand in HIS HOLY *PLACE* , the mountain. They could worship *God* in *quietness* , and could come *before* Him and receive *blessing* from Him.

Why was it that the theme of the first human couple coming to worship God on the Holy Mountain was so important to the early Chinese that they repeated it in many meaningful characters? Perhaps we can learn the reason as we continue our study.

CHAPTER 6

MORE ON THE NATURE OF *SHANGTI*

How delighted Adam and Eve must have been with their beautiful surroundings in the Garden of Eden! Their loving Creator-Father, *ShangTi,* had provided everything for their comfort and benefit. On every hand were luscious fruit-bearing trees and gorgeous flowers of many colors. Four sparkling rivers streamed from the sides of a magnificent mountain in the very center of the Garden, God's earthly dwelling place.

Eden's special mountain visited by *ShangTi* becomes more intriguing as we consider additional characters related to it. In the Hebrew scripture, God's place of *rest* (B)(止), or dwelling *place,* is called the "hill of the Lord" or "His holy place."

to rest

Let us consider some additional ancient forms of

mountain

mountain $\mathbf{W}$ (B)[1], $\square$ (O)[2]; $\mathbf{\dot{W}}$ (B)[3]; $\mathbf{W}$ (O)[4] (山). These are especially significant because of their similarity to the radicals for *fire* on the Oracle Bones: $\mathbf{\dot{W}}$(O)[5]; $\mathbf{W}$(O)[6]; $\mathbf{W}$(O).[7] From this we can assume that GOD'S GLORIOUS HOLY PRESENCE, AS DESIGNATED BY *FIRE*, ENSHROUDED HIS HOLY *MOUNTAIN*.

fire

Notice a character for *sun* $\mathbf{F}\overset{\circ}{\jmath}$ (B)[8] (陽) in which the brilliance of the *sun* $\odot$ is credited to *God* $\mathbf{J}$ on the *mount* $\mathbf{F}$ (阝) where God's presence Ξ is manifested.

$$\mathbf{F} \quad + \quad \odot \quad + \quad \mathbf{J} \quad = \quad \mathbf{F}\overset{\circ}{\jmath}$$

mount   sun   God   sun

sun

(Compare the first *adult male's* $\bullet$ "glory" in the character, *dawn* $\mathbf{\varphi}$ (旦 , p. 25), with *God's sunlike* $\overset{\circ}{\jmath}$ glory in *sun* $\mathbf{F}\overset{\circ}{\jmath}$.)

mount

In addition to the $\mathbf{F}$ form of *mount* seen above, there are several other variations of this radical: $\mathbf{\xi}$ (B)[9]; $\mathbf{\xi}$ (B)[10]; $\mathbf{\xi}$ (B)[11]. Each of these designate three *mouths* $\mathbf{\xi}$, $\mathbf{\xi}$, $\mathbf{\xi}$, or three *Persons* on the *mount*. (Again, notice the "blackening" of two of the symbols, indicating "holy"). Compare also the character, *hill* 阝, 陵(p. 51). Once more we observe a reference to the three Persons of the Godhead. From the Hebrew scriptures we learn that

mouth,
Person

the great God of creation was actually manifest in three forms: the FATHER, SON AND SPIRIT. Do the ancient Chinese bear out the same idea? Let us see.

Father

The *Father* 㕜 (父) has already been described and evidently took part in the creation of Adam (p. 30) and Eve (p. 36). We find the SPIRIT of God was also mentioned at the time of creation:

> In the beginning God created the heavens and the earth. And the earth was without form, and void; and darkness was upon the face of the deep; and the SPIRIT OF GOD was moving over the face of the water.[12]

Compare this further description of the SPIRIT'S activity in life and death:

> When you take away their BREATH,
>   they die and return to dust.
> When you send your SPIRIT,
>   they are created,
>   and you renew the face of the earth.[13]

We discover here that the "breath of life" is given by God's SPIRIT, and when withdrawn, death occurs. So when Adam was formed from the dust of the ground, and God *breathed* into his nostrils the breath of life, it was God's SPIRIT that gave the life.

> Then the Lord God took some soil from the ground and formed a man out of it; he BREATHED LIFE-GIVING BREATH

into his nostrils and the man began to live.[14]

The very character for *Spirit*  (S)[15] (靈) is most enlightening regarding the nature of God, so let us dissect it. First of all, we find *God* T on the mountain ⌐ (山) where the River of Life is represented by *water* 非 (水) descending. Observe especially the three *mouths, Persons* ᵥᵥᵥ , again suggesting the three Personalities of God who is a *worker of magic*  (巫) in His creative activity. *God's* work ⏌ (B)[16] (工) was *finished* ╎ (十) with the creation of two *persons* ⸜ and ⸝ , Adam and Eve.

T + ⌐ + 非 = ⊟ᴿ + ᵥᵥᵥ + 工 + ⸜⸝ =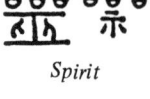

God   mountain water   rain   mouths   work   persons SPIRIT
              (River)   (three)   (two)

In one Bronzeware form, 霝 (B)[17], observe that this character does indeed represent the SPIRIT of God, for we find contained in it the *God radical* 示 .

God's SPIRIT has been identified with the "breath of life." How meaningful that an ancient figure for *breath* ≡ (O)[18] (气) shows THREE STROKES! We have just seen these three strokes ≡ in the radical, *mount* ᖴ . Recall, too, that ≡ are equated with *mouths, Persons* 𝍢 , as in 𝍢 , *mount*. THUS IT WOULD SEEM CONCLUSIVE THAT

Spirit

water

worker of magic

rain

work

breath

THE THREE STROKES ≡ ALSO REPRESENT THE THREE PERSONS OF THE TRINITY, CONSEQUENTLY, "GOD'S PRESENCE." Both Hebrew and Chinese sources disclose that the "breath of life" was given by God (the Trinity). Examine a second form of *breath* ≒ (B)[19] (气) which likewise depicts the holy mountain ㄱ .

A somewhat similar character, indicating *perfect* (O)[20] (全), portrays the combined *God* T and *breath* (Trinity) ≡ symbols, emphasizing God's *perfection.* The shape of Ω suggests the *Fountain* 瓜 (p. 46).

perfect

T	+	≡	+	Ω	=	全
God		*breath* (Trinity)		*fountain*		*perfect*

A discussion of the "God radicals," so frequently cited, is now timely. Anciently there were multiple forms, the most simple being T (O)[21] (示 , 礻 , 示). The figure, 示 (O)[21], containing a *water* 川 symbol, may be found duplicated in a later rendition, 川 (U)[22] (e.g. 川, p. 38). The *water* 川 (水) most likely represents the River of Life, which took origin on the Holy Mount, and is symbolic of God's life-giving propensity. Note especially the three strokes 川 . In the character 沛 (p. 50), we can see the God radical

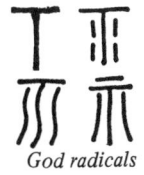
God radicals

川 ingeniously united with other features of the figure, and once again picturing the River descending from the Holy Mount 人 .

religion, belief, ancestral

We may well stand amazed at the knowledge of the venerable Chinese concerning the mystery of the Godhead! From the character 宗 (B)[23] , (宗) indicating *religion, belief in* and *ancestral,* we may gather that the original religious beliefs of the Chinese centered about the Triune God 示 of Heaven. They surely must have known that their *ancestral religion—* the faith of the very first *home* 宀 (宀), Adam and Eve's—was a belief in *ShangTi.* Apparently the Chinese patriarchs wanted to preserve forever precious knowledge regarding China's original God, as they perceived Him, with their concept of the Trinity.

home

In an early form of *home* 家 (B)[24] (家), we observe that, in the beginning, God was the head of the home. This figure 家 portrays *God, Heaven* 天 (天), as well as the *Father* 父 (父).

天	+	父	+	宀	=	家
God		Father		roof		home

It happens that in the evolution of the character for *home,* we find a duplication of what has happened in the homes of China. In a later form, 家 (U)[25] , we find the God of Heaven missing—forgotten! Only the ancestral *pair* Ⴒ + ⳾ remains.

Unfortunately, the first close relationship between *ShangTi* and His beloved human couple changed. This deviation we will find distinctly reflected in the venerable pictographs of the next chapters.

CHAPTER **7**

THE LETHAL BITE

> *The Master said, "Without recognizing the ordinances of HEAVEN, it is impossible to be a superior man.*
> *"Without an acquaintance with the rules of Propriety, it is impossible for the character to be established.*
> *"Without knowing THE FORCE OF WORDS, it is impossible to know men." CONFUCIAN ANALECTS, Bk. XX, Chap. III.*

There is no doubt that a tender relationship existed originally between *ShangTi* (*Shen*) and man! This loving bond is shown by a further style of writing *Shen*, (B)[1] (神). The *couple* + (the second "person" being upside down), are seen cleverly united in the symbol. How this first couple

God (Shen)

to instruct

must have enjoyed and looked forward to conversation with and *instruction* ⟨ 申 ⟩ from their Creator who desired to be identified so intimately with them that they became a part of His name!

$$ 示 \quad + \quad (\quad + \quad) \quad = \quad 示 $$

God radical   *to instruct*   *God (Shen)*

wedged between

In the character *to be wedged between* 夾 $_{(O)}$[2] (夾), this close relationship is quite obvious, for we recognize God, as a great, noble Being with arms outstretched 大, *"wedged between"* Adam and Eve, + .

$$ 大 \quad (大) \quad + \quad (\quad) \quad = \quad 夾 $$

noble Being (God)   *two persons*   *to be wedged between*

Sad events took place which destroyed these ties, separating Adam and Eve from their kind and beneficent Creator. In their many talks together, *ShangTi* had *instructed* $_{(B,O)}$[3] (申) Adam and Eve concerning an enemy, a mighty angel, called Lucifer. This angel had rebelled against God's fair government of love in heaven.

Scenes of what took place regarding Lucifer in heaven are recorded by inspiration in the Hebrew scriptures:

This is what the Sovereign Lord says:
"You [Lucifer] were the model of
perfection, full of wisdom and perfect
in beauty.
You were in EDEN, THE GARDEN OF
GOD [in heaven]...
You were anointed as a guardian cherub,
for so I ordained you.
You were blameless in your ways from the
day you were created till wickedness
was found in you...
So I drove you in disgrace from the mount
of God, and I expelled you, O guardian
cherub, from among the fiery stones.
YOUR HEART BECAME PROUD on
account of your beauty, and you cor-
rupted your wisdom because of your
splendor.
So I THREW YOU TO THE EARTH..."[4]

Again, we learn more of Lucifer, "the Morning
Star":

How you have fallen from heaven, O
Morning Star, son of the dawn!
YOU HAVE BEEN CAST DOWN TO THE
EARTH...
You said in your heart,
"I will raise my throne above the stars of
God;
I will sit enthroned on the mount of
assembly, on the utmost heights of the
SACRED MOUNTAIN.
I will ascend above the tops of the clouds;
I WILL MAKE MYSELF LIKE THE
MOST HIGH."[5]

Lucifer was not satisfied with his highest
position among the angels. He wanted to be a god

himself! He was consumed by jealousy at the creative power of *Shen* in the formation of our earth. So he inspired a mass discontent among the angels of heaven. Lucifer spread false accusations against *ShangTi,* saying that God was a cruel tyrant. As a result, one third of the angels of heaven joined Lucifer (also called Satan and the Devil) in this rebellion. We turn once again to the Hebrew record:

> Now war arose in heaven, Michael and his angels fighting against the dragon; and the dragon and his angels fought, but they were defeated and there was no longer any place for them in heaven. And the great dragon was thrown down, THAT ANCIENT SERPENT, who is called the DEVIL or SATAN, the deceiver of the whole world— he was THROWN DOWN TO THE EARTH, and his angels were thrown down with him.[6]

There was no doubt that Lucifer would try to gain Adam and Eve as his allies in his great controversy with *ShangTi.* One thing we should note in the above Hebrew narratives. Heaven, where God's throne is located on His "sacred mountain," is also called "the Garden of Eden." So we learn from this, that the GARDEN OF EDEN WHICH GOD PREPARED FOR ADAM AND EVE IN THE NEWLY CREATED EARTH WAS ACTUALLY A MINIATURE OF HEAVEN ITSELF!

As *ShangTi* talked daily with Adam and Eve on

His holy mountain in the earthly Garden of Eden, He had forbidden access to one tree in the Garden. It was called the "Tree of the Knowledge of Good and Evil." Fruit from this tree was not theirs to eat or even touch. God had imposed this one small, but important, test upon them to prove their loyalty to Him as their Creator and Benefactor.

God had *warned* and *admonished* the couple to *refrain from* 对(O)[7] (戒) eating the fruit of this forbidden tree. *God* 丁 *warned* them repeatedly not to take (pictured by a *hand* ㇕) the fruit of this tree 朿 .

to warn,
refrain from

丁	+	㇕	+	朿	=	对
God		hand (take)		tree		to warn, refrain from

Even before Eve was created on the sixth day of the first week, God had cautioned Adam:

> "You are free to eat from any tree in the garden, but you must not eat from the Tree of the Knowledge of Good and Evil; when you eat of it, you will surely die."[8]

In the character, *restrict, prevent, stop* 朿土(B)[9] (杜), the *tree* 朿 must definitely refer to the forbidden tree, for in this character, we find the newly created *adult male* ● of "dust" 土 to whom the

to restrict,
prevent

65

restriction had been addressed. How very accurate the Chinese writing is, for Eve is not included in the character, as she had not yet been created! She, of course, learned of the limitation later, for it applied to both of them.

forbid, warn

Yet another character, *to forbid, warn* 禁 (U)[10] (禁), gives additional details regarding God's 示 *command.* You will remember that this mysterious "Tree of the Knowledge of Good and Evil" stood next to the "Tree of Life" 林 in the middle of the Garden. In 禁 we see that the trees are located on the *mountain* 冂 (山), which is cleverly formed in the pictogram by extension of the tree roots.

straightforward

God had surely been *straightforward* 侃 (B)[11] (侃) in His admonition to the couple. In this character, God is represented by 彡 (see ☰ p. 57); 亻 portrays *man,* and the *mouth* 口 depicts His talking.

彡	+	口	+	亻 (亻)	=	侃
God		*mouth (talking)*		*man*		*straightforward*

imperial decree

God's word and instruction, however lovingly given, were no less than an *imperial decree* 旨 (B)[12] (旨) from the *mouth* 口 of the great *Being* 匕 (匕), the Ruler of the Universe! And it was a DEATH DECREE, should they fail to prove loyal to His kingdom of love.

One day as Eve had become separated from her husband, she passed through the center of the Garden. Suddenly she heard an unfamiliar voice. It was not Adam or *ShangTi* speaking. Who could it be? The voice seemed to come from the branches of the Tree of the Knowledge of Good and Evil. She *stopped* 休(B)[13] (休), intrigued and curious. Eve, the *person* 亻(亻), stood at the *Tree* 木 of the Knowledge of Good and Evil. There, sure enough, in its branches was a beautiful serpent—and it was he who was talking!

to stop

But just who was this addressing the unsuspecting Eve, disguised as a serpent? It was none other than *ShangTi's* enemy, that OLD SERPENT, Lucifer, the *devil* 鬼(O)[14](鬼), well symbolized in this radical. We find he is characterized as a *foreigner* 夷(O)[15](夷) to the *garden* 田 . What a correct portrayal!

devil

A Bronzeware depiction of the *devil* 鬼(B)[16] (鬼) has a slightly different twist, but nevertheless equally suitable. This time the *garden* ⊕ *man* 亻 covers his *mouth* with his hand 口 (口). This has been transcribed quite well into the modern character where 厶 indicates *secret*. The devil was, indeed, a "secret garden man!"

foreigner

⊕	+	亻	+	口	=	鬼
garden		*man*		*mouth*		*devil*

The Lethal Bite

The devil had waited for just this opportunity to approach Eve when she was alone. It was his plan to tempt her *privately* 厶 with his persuasive argument. The devil began a conversation by asking, "Did God really tell you not to eat fruit from any tree in the Garden?"[17] Eve answered, showing that she understood exactly the restrictions God had made:

"We may eat the fruit of any tree in the Garden except the Tree in the middle of it. God told us not to eat the fruit of that Tree or even touch it; if we do, WE WILL DIE."[18]

But the devil scoffingly answered:

"YOU WILL NOT SURELY DIE. For God knows that when you eat of it your eyes will be opened, and you will be like God, knowing good and evil."[19]

Eve was soon convinced that she need not fear death and that God was intentionally withholding good from them. She looked upon the fruit of the forbidden *tree* 木 and *desired, coveted* 林女 (O)[20] (婪) it. This character records that it was not man, but the *woman* 克 (O)[21] (女) who initially distrusted ShangTi and disregarded His *warning*

So she took of its fruit and ate.[22]

This sad waymark in the life of mankind is memorialized by another character for *beginning*

desire, covet

woman

始 (O) [23] (始), this time indicating the *BEGINNING OF SIN*. Here is seen a *woman* 𛀂 *secretly* 𛀂 eating, symbolized by the *mouth* 凵 . There is no mistaking the intent in another stylized form, (U) [24] which shows the symbol for *secretly, alone* 𛀂 (厶) dropping like a fruit into the open *mouth* 凵 (口) of the *woman* 𛀂 (女).

始

beginning

𛀂 (𛀂)	+	𛀂	+	凵	=	始
woman		*secretly*		*mouth (eating)*		*beginning*

𛀂 𛀂

secretly

And she also gave some to her husband and he ate.[25]

Both Adam and Eve had quickly fallen into the devil's cleverly planned trap!

Then the eyes of both were opened, and they knew that they were naked.[26]

They had been tricked! They soon realized that their understanding had not been broadened to their benefit, but to their great loss. As the glorious light signifying their sinless perfection and resemblance to God began fading, they discovered their nakedness. Hastily they "sewed fig leaves together and covered themselves."[27]

In their shame at being naked, and knowing that *ShangTi* would soon be visiting them, they quickly

clothes

made clothes of fig leaves. *Clothes* 仐 (O)[28] (衣), is a simple radical in which we find Adam 人 and Eve 尸. (Eve's origin from Adam's side 彡 is pictured). But when we look at a later writing, 衁 (U)[29] for *clothes* we see the *couple* 从 (衁), more clearly. We also observe that they are alone at the *mountain* 人 (山). God is not present. In a matter of a few minutes, Lucifer had accomplished his goal of separating the human family from *ShangTi*. The devil substituted distrust and suspicion for loyalty and love to the Heavenly Parent.

naked

A second word (see 夲 p. 28) for *naked* 裸 (U)[30] (裸) designates *fruit* 果 from the *garden* ⊞ of Eden as a reason for man's nakedness.

fruit

⊞	+	朮	=	果	+	仐	=	裸
garden		*tree*		*fruit*		*clothes*		*naked*

By their disobedient act of intentionally eating the *fruit* from the forbidden tree, they would lose access to the *fruit* from the Tree of Life. This second special Tree provided immortality as long as they regularly ate of its fruit. It had been God's plan that they eat daily of the Tree of Life, and live forever. Therefore, it would seem that "fruit" 果 is a very appropriate symbol to describe their plight of *nakedness.*

It would soon be time for *ShangTi's* daily visit and *descent from heaven*  (B)[31] (降). This interesting pictogram shows "movement," for there are both of God's feet ↑ , in constrast to a single foot, meaning *stop, rest* (p. 41). Also notice that the direction of the feet are downward, indicating the descent.

descent from heaven, to descend

God is *coming down* to His sacred *mount* (p. 54). He, of course, already knew what had happened. As He looked at their hastily put-together fig-leaf garments, He asked,

> "Did you eat the fruit that I told you not to eat?"[32]

There followed a series of accusations and excuses:

> The man answered, "The woman you put here with me gave me the fruit, and I ate it." . . . She replied, "The snake tricked me into eating it."[33]

Already Adam and Eve had taken on characteristics of the great *accuser,* Lucifer. Another form of *devil* (B)[34] (鬼) (see p. 67) shows Lucifer, the devil, , coming before God , to *accuse* (symbolized by a mouth) Adam and Eve of disobeying God's command.

devil

God spoke first to Lucifer, who became known as "the old serpent," "the devil," and the "dragon:"

> "And I will put enmity [hatred] between

> you and the woman, and between your
> seed and her SEED; He shall bruise your
> head, and you shall bruise His heel."[35]

In this curse put upon His foe, Lucifer, the devil, *ShangTi* PRONOUNCED FOR THE FIRST TIME A WONDERFUL PLAN FOR MAN'S ULTIMATE SALVATION. Through the later descendants of the woman would eventually come a SAVIOR (the promised "SEED"). He would crush and utterly defeat the devil and his angels. But in so doing, the SAVIOR would suffer great agony on behalf of the guilty human race. This SAVIOR WAS ONE OF THE GODHEAD, THE "SON," who would one day come as a human being to earth.

Next, *ShangTi* addressed Eve:

> "I will greatly multiply your SORROW
> and your conception; in pain you shall
> bring forth children; your desire shall be
> for your husband, and he shall rule over
> you."[36]

Doubtless God had originally intended the bearing of children to be a completely joyful experience. However the bodily deterioration which womankind would suffer as the result of sin would no longer permit this. Pain would become the lot of women in childbirth. From this time on, the husband would rule over the wife. She would fall from her original position as his equal.

Eve's *sorrow* (O)[37] (楚) depicts again the site at the *Trees* 艸. We see the woman represented by both a *mouth* ○ (口) which she used to eat the fruit of the forbidden Tree, and also by a foot, where she unwittingly *stopped* ㅂ (止). In a second form (B)[38], the act of stealing the fruit is pinpointed by a *person's* very large arm ㅈ reaching out toward one tree 木 to grasp a *piece* ㅌ (疋). There is no mistaking Eve standing with outstretched hand below the two trees in this word for *sorrow* . But one must understand the original history, as did the venerable inventor of the written language, in order to interpret it correctly.

sorrow

But what of Adam? His "sorrow" is also specific. Said God:

> "CURSED IS THE GROUND because of
>   you; through painful toil you will eat of
>   it all the days of your life . . .
> By the sweat of your brow
>   you will eat your food
> until you RETURN TO THE GROUND,
>   since from it you were taken;
> for dust you are
>   and TO DUST YOU WILL RETURN."[39]

From the character meaning *difficult, trouble, worry* (O)[40] (困), we can easily understand how eating from the forbidden *Tree* 木 (木) in the garden *enclosure* □ was the beginning of all their *difficulties* and *trouble.*

trouble, worry

death

God had pronounced the sure penalty of *death* 佨 (O)[41] (死) for the disobedience of eating the forbidden fruit. God on his holy mount 丹 is depicted, pronouncing the *death* penalty for guilty man 亻 .

卜 (𠂇) + 丹 + 亻 (𠂆) = 佨

God   mount   man   death

death

A second oracle bone inscription for this character, *death,* is 囚 (O)[42] (死), which shows a *noble* 大 man in the Garden *enclosure* ☐ . Adam, that man, would suffer death. The fact that Adam and Eve lived on after their disobedience makes us realise that the death was ultimate, and that they no longer had immortality. Spiritual death, however, was immediate, for they were cut off from God's presence, and could no longer appear face-to-face before Him. Thus sin separated mankind from their sinless God.

Now God had declared that Adam would return to the ground,

> "Since from it you were taken; for dust you are, and to dust you will return."[43]

How true the familiar Chinese saying. *"In the beginning man's original character was virtuous"* 人之 初性本善. Unfortunately, man's perfect, sinless character was lost by a single willful act. Adam had eaten the forbidden fruit offered him by his wife, knowing full well that he was disobeying the expressed command of his loving, kind Creator. HE HAD LISTENED TO THE WORDS OF HIS WIFE AND THE DEVIL ABOVE GOD'S WARNING. This resulted in their alienation from God, the source of all life. The separation of Adam and Eve from the Life-Giver meant DEATH, an inescapable consequence. They had forfeited immortality. And they had brought it upon themselves!

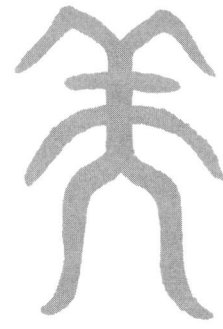

CHAPTER 8

A COSTLY
RESCUE PLAN

The devil claimed that God was a tyrant! If at this point *ShangTi* had abandoned Adam and Eve as hopeless rebels who could not even observe the smallest and simplest request possible, we might have to agree with the devil. But God did not leave His beloved Adam and Eve without hope. Already He had provided a SAVIOR in the promised SEED of the woman. Now He wanted to explain more of the coming SAVIOR'S love for lost mankind.

ShangTi viewed the miserable fig leaf *clothes* 衣 (衣) Adam and Eve had fashioned for themselves (p. 70). A costly and symbolic demonstration followed

clothes

as the lives of innocent animals were sacrificed to provide skins to RECLOTHE the sorrowing couple.

> The Lord God made garments of skin for Adam and his wife and clothed them.[1]

Never before had they witnessed the awfulness of death. Their beautiful animal friends were killed to symbolize the death of God's sinless SON, One of the Godhead, who would come to earth as a human being and ultimately give His life for mankind.

This great act of clothing Adam and Eve with the skins of the sacrificial animals carries deep meaning and is memorialized in several characters. It was the *BEGINNING* 衩 (O)[2] (初) of the PLAN OF SALVATION for mankind. The symbolic *clothes* 衣 of skins for the guilty pair were provided only by the slaying of animals with a *knife* 刂 (刀).

beginning

robes

The new *robes* 袞 (O)[3] (袁) were a gift from God 火 . Here *God* 屮 is melded with His holy *mountain* 𠆢 (Compare with 图 , p. 47). Again we find the united *persons* 从 who are symbolically *clothed* 衣 with the righteous character of the promised SON.

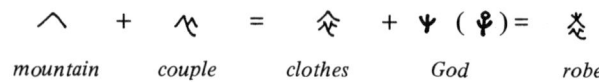

𠆢	+	从	=	衣	+	屮 (𡴪) =	袞
mountain		*couple*		*clothes*		*God*	*robe*

Another character also using the significant radical, *clothes* 衣 , is *to forgive, depend on, lean on* 依 (O)[4] (依). Inserted into the radical is the great *Being* 大 , God, whose provision of *garments* 衣 for the man and his wife ∀ brought *forgiveness,* and was meant to teach Adam and Eve that they needed to *depend on* 依 Him for hope of salvation from eternal death.

forgive, depend on

∧ + ∀ = 衣 + 大 (大) = 依

mount　　couple　　clothes　　Being (God)　　forgive, depend on

to die

Innocent animals had *to die* 卒 (O)[5] (卒) so that *clothes* 衣 could be provided by God's *hand* 手 (手). It is likely that the creatures sacrificed were *sheep* 羊 (B)[6] (羊), for this animal above all others was to represent God's own SON who was later to be called "the Lamb of God who takes away the sin of the world."[7]

righteousness

In the character for *righteousness* 義 (B)[8] (義), we also find the *sheep* 羊 , like a garment, covering over *"me"* 我 (我). But *"me"* is composed of a *hand* 手 (手) and *spear, lance* 戈 (戈)—which tells the story that *"I"* am responsible for the death of the *Lamb* 羊 , (by my sins), for my *hand* holds the killing instrument.

hand

spear, lance

me

奻 + 𠂤 = 義 + 羊 = 義

hand   lance   me   sheep   righteousness

beautiful

Originally it was Adam whose sins were covered by the righteous "Lamb 羊 of God." We discover this in the character *beautiful* 𣥹 (O)[9] (美), for the *noble man* 大 , Adam is pictographically portrayed. Eve, the *woman* 𠨰 (女), was also included, however, in some renditions of the character, as 𣥹 (O).[10] When the Lamb covered their sins, they were indeed *beautiful* in God's eyes, for He could see only His sinless Son, represented by the *Lamb* 羊 .

sheep

The Hebrew record next states:

> And the Lord God said, "The man has now become like one of us, knowing good and evil. HE MUST NOT BE ALLOWED TO REACH OUT HIS HAND AND TAKE ALSO FROM THE TREE OF LIFE AND EAT, AND LIVE FOREVER." So the Lord God banished him from the Garden of Eden to work the ground from which he had been taken. After he drove the man out, he placed on the east side of the Garden of Eden cherubim [angels] and a flaming sword flashing back and forth TO GUARD THE WAY TO THE TREE OF LIFE.[11]

Interestingly, in one of the ancient books of the *Chou* dynasty, it is recorded: "Because MAN SINNED IN ANCIENT TIMES, the God of Heaven

[天帝] ordered *Chung* and *Li* to BLOCK UP THE WAY BETWEEN HEAVEN AND EARTH."[12] Perhaps *"Chung"* and *"Li"* were the two angels on either side of Eden's gate!

So God expelled Adam and Eve from the Garden. As they passed through the eastern Garden *gate* ⸢(O)⸣[13](門), they realized that this meant their exclusion from the life-giving Tree of Life and immortality. Note the *hands* ⸢ and the barrier ⊢ blocking the *gate* entrance. A *barrier, fence* ⸢(B)⸣[14](閑) had been set up past which they could not go to eat from the *Tree* ⸢ of Life. There were two angels [cherubim] guarding the way. Instead of *hands* ⸢ at the *gate* entrance, some ancient forms depict "the presence of God" ⸢(U) .[15] It seems, therefore, that the *gate* of Eden became the new place of worshiping God, since sin had prevented a face-to-face visit with God on the Holy Mount inside the Garden.

gate

barrier, fence

Adam and Eve, now turned out of the Garden, felt *alone* ⸢(B)⸣[16](單). The conjoined *couple* ⸢ are depicted OUTSIDE the *Garden* ⊕ . It was time for them to *think* and *meditate* ⸢(U)⸣[17](禪), not about their punishment, but about the goodness of *God* ⸢ in spite of their ungrateful disloyalty. For God had provided *garments* ⸢(U)⸣[18](襌) for the unworthy *couple* ⸢ , even though cast out of their

alone

think, meditate

Garden ⊕ home.

garments

❦	+	⊕	=	❦	+	⩗	=	❦
couple		*garden*		*alone*		*clothes*		*garments*

⌀❦ has an interesting secondary meaning of *leveling an area for an altar.* This was probably one of their first undertakings, for as they found themselves in *strange* and *unfamiliar* ❦ (O) [19] (異) surroundings, they felt their need of communion with God. Depicted OUTSIDE the *Garden* ⊕ is a kneeling figure ❦ with upraised hands, a characteristic posture of worship. A second form of this character, *strange* ❦ (B) [20], reveals CONJOINED hands ❦ , which would suggest that the hands of both worshipers are represented.

strange, unfamiliar

❦ (❦ + ❦) +		⊕	=	❦
hands		*Garden*		*strange*

to seek, pray

We see them *seeking, praying to* ❦ (B) [21] (覲) God. The first *two persons* ❦ are found OUTSIDE the boundary of the Garden ❦ , while inside is *God on the mount* ❦ where the *River* of Life ⼮ streams down the mountain side.

❦	+	❦	+	❦ (❦)+	❦	+	⼮	=	❦
couple		*garden (boundary)*		*God*	*mount*		*River*		*to seek, pray*

82

The Garden *gate* Þ⁣ ⁣⁣ was the site where they came to *ask* and *inquire* ᛒ (O)²² (問) of God concerning their needs.

Þ⁣ ⁣⁣	+	ᛒ	=	ᛒ
gate		*mouth*		*ask, inquire*

to ask, inquire

An unblemished *Lamb* 𦍙 (B)²³ (羔), symbolizing the SAVIOR to come, was sacrificed and burned at the gate. Animal *sacrifices* (O)²⁴ (祀) became an important part of their worship. The pictogram reveals the *person* 𠂤 ( ) bending in obeisance, and offering with a *hand* something to *God* T. A Bronzeware figure for the same character, *sacrifice* (B)²⁵, portrays a person kneeling before *God* . That the offering to God was always made OUTSIDE the Garden is quite obvious in yet another form of the same character, (U)²⁶, where we see the same conjoined *hands* as in *strange, unfamiliar* above, indicating TWO + worshipers.

lamb

to sacrifice

A second character for *sacrifice* (B)²⁷ (祭) also has ancient roots. Here we recognize the *hand* serving *God* . Recall the radical 夕 (and , p. 37, as well as and , p. 50), meaning *vessel* (舟), which pictures two bowing persons ( ). This radical is often exchanged with *flesh* (肉).

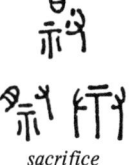

sacrifice

Either one could be equally well substituted, for in *flesh* 创 , the two persons are likewise represented (创 , p. 34).

𝄞　(ทٴٴ)　+　Ч　+　示　=　創

vessel (two persons)　　　　　hand　　　God　　　to sacrifice
(flesh (two persons))

Oracle Bone inscriptions of *sacrifice* 祠 , 禄 (O)[28] clearly reveal *two hands* 臼 , 与 of two worshipers of God 丅 , 示 . Communion is depicted by the *mouth* 廿 .

sacrificial animals

The sheep was not the only animal used in the worship of *ShangTi*, for the character, *sacrificial animals* 犠 (U)[29] (犠), shows not only a *sheep* 羊 , but also a *bullock, ox* 牛 (牛). The instrument for killing the animals was a *lance, spear* 戈 (戈). Futhermore, we learn from this character that the animals must be *"beautiful"* 秀 (秀), unblemished, or perfect. Only thus could they symbolize the sinless SON of God to come. We can compare this Chinese pictograph with the instruction given by God to the Hebrews:

> "Take a BULL CALF for a sin offering, and a RAM for a burnt offering, both WITHOUT BLEMISH, AND OFFER THEM BEFORE THE Lord."[30]

The character, *sacrificial animals* 犧 , has the same phonetic sound, *hsi*, as *evening* 夕 and *west* 西 . It would certainly suggest that the word for "sacrificial animals," arose phonetically by association with the time of the ritual in the evening. *To sacrifice* 祀 (祀), on the other hand, also designates a time—9-11 a.m. Thus, it would seem, that the early Chinese had two daily sacrifices—morning and evening. We can compare these Chinese pictographs with the instruction given by God to the Hebrews:

> One lamb you shall offer in the morning, and the other lamb you shall offer in the evening.[31]

The combined information gained from both the Chinese and Hebrew sources also amplifies the story related in the Hebrew record regarding the sacrifices offered years later by Adam's first two sons, Cain and Abel:

> Now Abel kept flocks, and Cain worked the soil. In the course of time Cain brought some of the fruits of the soil as an offering to the Lord. But Abel brought fat portions from some of the first born of his flock. The Lord looked with favor on Abel and his offering, but on Cain and his offering he did not look with favor. So Cain was very angry, and his face was downcast.[32]

We can understand that Cain was not bringing a

proper sacrifice. His fruits of the soil had no life, no meaning, no symbolism of a coming SAVIOR. God could not accept them. Cain had a rebellious spirit. He wanted his own way of worship. He was unwilling to accept God's plan. In a fit of jealousy because Abel's offering of a lamb had been accepted, he killed his brother.

cruel, fierce

The Oracle Bone inscriptions record this *cruel, violent, fierce* act of murder in the character 兇 (o) [33] (兇). We see Cain pictured as the *elder brother* (兄) who is taking hold of his younger brother, Abel (儿). Note that there is a mark × on Cain, for in the Hebrew Scriptures it is recorded:

elder brother

> And the Lord put a MARK on Cain, lest any who came upon him should kill him. [34]

When the Lord drove Cain from that place to become a fugitive in the earth, it is written that "Cain went out from the LORD'S PRESENCE." [35] He no longer worshiped at the *gate* of Eden where "God's presence" was manifested. Cain and his wife (his sister), became the ancestors of a rebellious race who hated God.

But there have been those in the history of the earth, as men multiplied, who appreciated the God of Heaven. It was these who kept alive a knowledge of Him and His wonderful plan for the salvation of all mankind. The Hebrews were one of these people, worshiping *El Shaddai* (p. 18). It appears that the ancient Chinese were other believers in the Creator, whom they called *ShangTi.*

Although a knowledge of *ShangTi* today has been largely lost in China, yet this sacred history of earth's beginnings was carefully recorded for all time in their ancient pictographic and ideographic writing. This cryptic information has been awaiting recovery, so that both oriental and occidental peoples might have confidence in *ShangTi (El Shaddai)* as the God of the Universe!

CHAPTER 9

UNRAVELING A CONFUCIAN PUZZLE

The new site for the worship of *ShangTi* was at the EAST GATE of the Garden of Eden. This we learn from the Chinese characters and also from the Hebrew record, which reads:

> He drove out the man; and at the EAST of the Garden of Eden he placed the cherubim [angels], and a flaming sword which turned every way, to guard the way to the Tree of Life.[1]

The radical, *gate* ᚦᚈ, (門, p. 81) shows not only God's *Hands* (compare ( ) p. 23; p. 27; p. 35) there, but His presence (℻, ᚠ pp. 50, 51; 三, 丌 pp. 56, 57) as well. The *gate* became a new HOLY PLACE.

The original *place* (所 , p. 51) of worship was on the *mountain* (compare , p. 54). That site, or *place* was the HOLY HILL, where Adam and Eve, in their original sinless state, could *meet* (O)[2] (見) God face-to-face, eye-to-*eye* (O)[3] (目), on bended knee as worshipers. Note how ingenious this pictogram of *eye* is, for the iris is actually the *sun* ⊙ with the pupil being the *flame of fire* · , or "glory." The *sun* ⊙ represented both God and man who was "made in God's image," (pp. 25, 26). It is recorded in the Hebrew Scriptures that God said,

to meet

eye

> ". . . he that touches you, touches the APPLE OF HIS [God's] EYE."[4]

The "apple of the eye" in the pictogram is the *sun* ⊙ .

After Adam and Eve had been expelled from Eden, the new location for worship, therefore, was at the Garden *boundary, BORDER* (O),[5] (O)[6] (圉). A *boundary* had been set up at the gate, a *barrier* , to keep the first couple from the Tree of

Life (p. 81). There are a number of Oracle Bone renditions for this character. Two have been selected in order to more accurately arrive at its meaning. In  , the worshiper is quite obvious as 𝄞 (𝄞). God is represented by 𝄞 , the legs of which are melded with the "horns" of a primitive *sheep* 𝄞 radical. The second character 𝄞 , does not show the worshiper, but a communication at the *BORDER* of the Garden *enclosure* ☐ is indicated by a *mouth* ☐ at the top of the God figure, as 𝄞 . The *sheep* 𝄞 sacrifice is clearly seen.

border, boundary

Eden's gate was now the *border* or *boundary* past which they were prevented going by the presence of the cherubim angels. There are many characters meaning *border* or *boundary*. All have the same reference, the BORDER of the Garden of Eden, more specifically, at the east gate.

The character meaning *frontier (border) gate* and also *to close, shut* 𝄞(O)[7] (關), shows two *adult male* ● *persons* ‖ , possibly referring to Adam and Seth, his son born after Abel's death and Cain's exile. These two 𝄞 stand at the *shut border gate* 𝄞 . Examine also an additional interpretation of the same character, 𝄞(U)[8], which indicates a communication, *mouth* ▽ (☐), at the *gate* ⌐ (門) between *two* ·· *persons* ♭ (compare 𝄞 , p. 40) and *God* ⊤ . The fact that God and the couple 𝄞 are joined suggests

frontier (border), gate, to shut

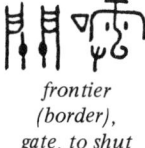

91

a close relationship between them. The upraised *hand* 𝒴 portrays worship.

$$\top + \ \cdots \ + \ \eth \ + \ \cap \ + \ \triangledown \ + \ 𝒴 \ = \ \text{(symbol)}$$

God	two	person(s)	gate	mouth (speaking)	hand (wor- shiping)	BORDER gate, to shut

border, to come before God

A third character for *BORDER*, (symbol)$_{(U)}$ [9] (畛), portrays Adam, a *person* 𝟋 bowing OUTSIDE the *Garden* ⊞ where God's presence 𝒴 is manifested. A secondary, rather archaic, meaning of this symbol is *to come before God.*

border

This is somewhat similar to the character, *BORDER, BOUNDARY* (symbol)$_{(U)}$ [10] (界) where *two* ıı *persons* 𝟋 are once more found OUTSIDE the *Garden* ⊞ .

How amazing that there are so many Chinese characters for BORDER, each of them denoting the BORDER OF EDEN: the *Garden* ⊞ , the Garden *enclosure* ☐ , the *gate* Þ ᑫ or in yet another, the Holy Mountain *BORDER* (symbol)$_{(B)}$ [11] (際)! This is not difficult to interpret.

border

$$ \text{(vessel)} \ (\text{刀厂}) + \ \text{(hand)} \ + \ \text{(God)} \ = \ \text{(SACRIFICE)} \ + \ \text{(mount)} \ = \ \text{(BORDER)} $$

vessel (two persons)	hand (worshiping)	God	SACRIFICE	mount	BORDER

92

However, no *sacrifice* 祭 ever took place on the Sacred Hill itself, as the Hebrew scriptures remind us:

> "They shall not hurt or destroy
> in all my holy mountain,"
> says the Lord.[12]

Therefore, the *mount* 丘 itself, as it rose majestic and beautiful in the center of the Garden, must have indicated the BORDER 邊祭 of Eden where the *sacrifice* took place.

WE MAY CONCLUDE THAT THIS DAILY SERVICE OUTSIDE OF EDEN'S EAST GATE, WAS A "BORDER SACRIFICE" INITIATED BY *SHANGTI,* HIMSELF. After Adam and Eve were driven from the Garden, they could ask forgiveness for sin by a symbolic animal sacrifice at the border or gate of the Garden of Eden. THE BORDER SACRIFICE AT EDEN'S CLOSED GATE LOOKED FORWARD TO THE SACRIFICE OF THE "SEED OF THE WOMAN" (p. 72) ON BEHALF OF ALL THE DESCENDANTS OF ADAM.

We should not get the idea of a bloodthirsty god, demanding appeasement! Far from it, God was to SACRIFICE His own SON for the benefit of mankind who were under the death penalty. Of God, the Hebrew writings make clear:

You do not delight in SACRIFICE, or I
   would bring it;
you do not take pleasure in burnt offerings.
The SACRIFICES of God are a broken
   spirit;
a broken and contrite heart,
O God, you will not despise.[13]

The great philosopher, Confucius, was a worshiper of *ShangTi.* He used his influence to preserve
the purity of the worship services to the God of
Heaven. However, Confucius himself did not understand the ancient system of sacrifice which took place
each year at the border of his country. In this Chinese
"BORDER SACRIFICE," recall that the emperor
alone, took a young, unblemished bull, slew it and
burned it upon an altar. The whole ceremony was
accompanied by music and recitations to *ShangTi*
(some of which have been quoted in the first three
chapters of this book.) The emperor concluded the
service by bowing low before the sacrificial altar in
worship of *ShangTi.*

We might digress momentarily to learn a bit
about the ancient sage, Confucius, who stands as
perhaps China's last guardian of original truth —
dimmed almost to extinction in his day.

In the *Confucian Analects* are snatches of information which paint a beautiful picture of the faith
and integrity of this noble man:

The Master said,

"At fifteen, I had my mind bent on
   learning.
At thirty, I stood firm.
At forty, I had no doubts.
At fifty, I knew the decrees of Heaven.
At sixty, my ear was an obedient organ for
   the reception of truth.
At seventy, I could follow what my heart
   desired, without transgressing what was
   right."[14]

His humility shines forth in these quotations:

The Master said, "The sage and the man of
perfect virtue;—how dare I rank myself
with them? It may be simply said of me,
that I strive to become such without
satiety, and teach others without weari-
ness."[15]

The Master said, "When I walk along with
two others, they may serve me as my
teachers. I will select their good qualities
and follow them, their bad qualities and
avoid them."[16]

The Master said, *"Heaven produced the
virtue that is in me."*[17]

Confucius was very interested in the ancient
sacrifice custom, realizing that there must be an
important significance to the ceremony. Therefore
he evidentally spent much time researching into its
true meaning. But finally Confucius had to admit:

> "... He who understands the ceremonies of the sacrifices to Heaven and Earth, ... would find the government of a kingdom as easy as to look into his palm! "[18]

In Confucius' day, about 500 B.C., at least 1700 years had already passed since the dynastic rule of China was established. The first rulers, it appears, understood the religious principles which had been handed down by word of mouth from the time of Creation. The ancient sage who had invented the written language also had true concepts of the history of the world. He recorded this knowledge for all time in his ideographic characters. The *Hsia* and *Shang* dynasties had passed, and now, during Confucius' lifetime, the famed *Chou* dynasty was ruling China.

Because of the long passage of time, therefore, a true knowledge of *ShangTi* had already been lost. The BORDER SACRIFICE relating to the worship of *ShangTi* had survived in name only, to become a mysterious ritual, a national custom of unknown significance and origin.

As we have briefly reviewed the history of Adam and Eve, we found that their unfortunate act of disobedience and disloyalty meant the death sentence. But *ShangTi* had proposed to ransom them by sending a SAVIOR to be born as the "SEED of the woman." In the plan, this SAVIOR would "crush the head of the serpent," that old enemy of God, the devil. However, the SAVIOR Himself would be "bitten in the heel." What did this mean?

When Adam and Eve left their beautiful Garden home, *ShangTi* had lovingly provided garments of skins for them. These *robes* 衮 (袁 , p. 78) made necessary the death of innocent sacrificial animals, likely *sheep* 羊 to cover their nakedness. The *Lamb* 羔 was another symbol of the coming SAVIOR. The sacrifice of this animal was to represent the SAVIOR'S death and payment for their sentence, "You will surely die." The sinless SAVIOR would substitute His life for sinful man.

robe

"You will not die," had been the devil's promise to Eve. Who would be right, *ShangTi* or the devil? Death has come upon all men, from Adam's son, Abel, the first to die, to our very day.

God had told Adam he would return to dust. Death is the opposite of creation, as we learned in a previously quoted Hebrew text:

> When you take away their breath,
>   they die and return to dust.
> When you send your Spirit,
>   they are created.[19]

Compare also:

> When his breath departs, he returns to his earth; in that very day, his plans perish.[20]

But is there no hope that the dead will ever live again? This is where *ShangTi's* wonderful plan of salvation comes in. God's own SON would one day be born as the SEED of the woman, live a sinless life and give His life for every man who allows himself to be covered by the *righteousness* 羕 (義 , p. 79) of this heavenly Sacrifice. There will be a day when all the righteous dead will live again, according to this Hebrew record:

righteousness

> And many of those who sleep in the dust of the earth shall awake, some to everlasting life, and some to shame and everlasting contempt. And those who are wise shall shine like the brightness of the firmament; and those who turn many to righteousness, like the stars for ever and ever.[21]

In Confucius' day, had that Supreme Sacrifice been made? Had the promised SEED of the woman, the SAVIOR of ALL mankind, yet come? Only about two hundred years before the time of Confucius, a Hebrew prophet had looked far down into the future. (But he had written in past tense as though the event had already happened). Listen to this highly descriptive and detailed picture which he related about the SAVIOR to come:

> Who would have believed what we now report? Who could have seen the Lord's hand in this?
> It was the will of the Lord that His Servant

grow like a plant [SEED] taking root in
dry ground . . .
We despised Him and rejected Him;
He endured suffering and pain.
No one would even look at Him—
We ignored Him as if He were nothing.
But He endured the suffering that should
have been ours, the pain we should have
borne . . .
BECAUSE OF OUR SINS HE WAS
WOUNDED, beaten because of the evil
we did.
We are healed by the punishment He
suffered, made whole by the blows He
received.
All of us were like sheep that were lost,
each of us going his own way.
But the Lord made the punishment fall on
Him, the punishment all of us deserved.
He was treated harshly, but endured it
humbly;
He never said a word.
He was arrested and sentenced and led off
to die, and no one cared about His fate.
HE WAS PUT TO DEATH FOR THE
SINS OF OUR PEOPLE.
He was placed in a grave with evil men,
he was buried with the rich,
even though He had never committed a
crime or ever told a lie.
The Lord says,
"It was my will that He should suffer
HIS DEATH WAS A SACRIFICE TO
BRING FORGIVENESS . . .
And through Him my purpose will succeed.
After a life of suffering, He will again
have joy,
He will know that He did not suffer in vain.
My devoted Servant, with whom I am
pleased, and for His sake I will forgive
them.

And so I will give Him a place of honor,
a place among great and powerful men.
He willingly gave His life and shared the
      fate of evil men.
HE TOOK THE PLACE OF MANY
      SINNERS
and prayed that they might be forgiven."[22]

No, in Confucius' day, the promise had not yet been fulfilled. The time was still in the future for *ShangTi's* purposes to be realized. Where was this promised SAVIOR to be born? What part of the world would be honored to have the SON of God in human form visit them?

The *Han* dynasty followed the famed *Chou* dynasty of Confucius' era. During the reign of Emperor *Ai* 哀帝 [23] (and perhaps his name was prophetic, "to pity, to sympathize with"), a son was born to a humble peasant couple, Joseph and Mary. They lived in a land far-distant from China. On a map, you may locate the country of Israel (today much in the news) to the east of the Mediterranean Sea. This was the ancient land of the Hebrews, whose venerable Scriptures we have been comparing with the Chinese character writing. In a small town of Bethlehem in the province of Judea an event of great importance to the WHOLE WORLD took place. But many strange things happened simultaneously with the birth of this Special Baby!

ALTAR OF HEAVEN, PEKING, WITH TEMPLE OF HEAVEN IN IMMEDIATE BACKGROUND

這是北平天壇全景，中間的建築物是祈年殿。

CHAPTER 10

THE SEED
OF THE WOMAN

The first in a series of strange events was the appearance of a heavenly angel to a lovely young woman, Mary, with an important message. Mary was looking forward to her approaching marriage with Joseph. Both were descendants of King David, in the royal Judean line. But it had been centuries since a Judean king had ruled over Israel. Indeed, at that time (nearly 2,000 years ago), their nation was under the tyrannical rule of Rome. Joseph was, instead of a prince, a humble carpenter in the town of Nazareth.

The visit of an angel was a rare event of great honor and the heavenly messenger put aside Mary's fears by saying:

> "Don't be afraid, Mary; God has been gracious to you. You will become pregnant and give birth to a SON and you will name Him JESUS. He will be great and will be called the SON OF THE MOST HIGH GOD. The Lord God will make Him a king, as his ancestor David was, . . . His kingdom will never end! "[1]

Mary was perplexed and said to the angel, "I am a virgin. How then, can this be?"

> "The angel answered, "The HOLY SPIRIT [one member of the Godhead] will come on you, and God's power will rest upon you. For this reason the Holy Child will be called the SON OF GOD" [a second member of the Godhead].[2] (See Chapter 6).

Mary responded, "I am the Lord's servant, may it happen to me as you have said."[3]

The angel also visited Joseph, reassuring him:

> "Joseph, descendant of David, do not be afraid to take Mary to be your wife. For it is by the HOLY SPIRIT that she has conceived. She will have a SON, and you will name Him JESUS—because HE WILL SAVE HIS PEOPLE FROM THEIR SINS."[4]

So Joseph had taken Mary as his wife. A few months later there was a great census being taken throughout the Roman empire. Everyone was required to register in the hometown of their family's ancestral leader. Thus Joseph and Mary journeyed to Bethlehem, the ancient town of their ancestor, King David.

Bethlehem, they found upon their arrival, was very crowded with travelers so that there were no empty inn rooms. The best they could do was to find a sleeping place on the sweet-smelling hay in a barn. It was under these humble conditions that Jesus, the long-awaited "SEED of the woman" was born to this poor peasant couple.

Predictions of a promised SAVIOR had been known to the human family since the time of Adam and Eve when they were expelled from the Garden of Eden. Yet how many expected Him at this time? In the Hebrew sacred writings, there were many prophecies foretelling of Jesus' coming to earth. Daniel, a prince and a prophet living as a captive in Babylon during Confucius' own lifetime, had written of the exact time when the SAVIOR would appear. But only a few had bothered to study the Hebrew Scriptures to learn when this might be. These faithful ones knew that His coming must be soon. Among the expectant believers were simple shepherds who often talked of the SAVIOR and what His coming would be like. As these herdsmen were watching their flocks in the countryside one night, an angel appeared to them also, joyously announcing:

> "Don't be afraid! I am here with GOOD
> NEWS for you, which will bring great joy
> to ALL THE PEOPLE. This very day in
> David's town your SAVIOR was born—
> Christ the Lord! And this is what will
> prove it to you. You will find a baby
> wrapped in cloths and lying in a manger."[5]

Then appeared to the amazed shepherds a great host of angels singing and rejoicing. They led them to where Mary, Joseph and the Baby were—not to a palace, but to an animal shed!

The newborn Baby had other visitors as well. THREE WISE MEN ARRIVED FROM THE ORIENT. They too had studied the prophecies of the Hebrew scriptures and had seen a beautiful moving star arise in the east. They had learned that a special star would be seen in the heavens to announce the birth of a SAVIOR. Therefore they determined to follow the star and had traveled a great distance. The star led them to Jerusalem where they inquired of the ruler, Herod, the whereabouts of the Baby born to be the King of the Jews. Herod was greatly upset. He called together the chief priests and teachers of the people to ask where the SAVIOR was to be born. They read for him the prophecy which had been written hundreds of years before:

Bethlehem Ephrathath, you are one of the smallest towns in Judah, but out of you I will bring a ruler for Israel, whose family line goes back to ancient times . . . When he comes, he will rule his people with the strength that comes from the Lord and with the majesty of the Lord God himself. His people will live in safety because PEOPLE ALL OVER THE EARTH WILL ACKNOWLEDGE HIS GREATNESS, and he will bring peace.[6]

Herod was so disturbed by this word that he determined to destroy the Baby who would possibly depose him from his throne. But not revealing his evil intentions, Herod said to the wise men, "Go and make careful search for the child; and when you find him, let me know, so that I too may go and worship him."[7]

Once more the star appeared, and the oriental sages followed it to the very place where the Baby Jesus was resting. The three visitors from the East entered the dwelling, and knelt before the Baby. They gave gifts of gold, frankincense and myrrh, which they had brought with them. These men were then warned in a dream not to return to Herod, so they left for their own country by another route.

Once more an angel appeared to Joseph with the warning to take his family immediately to Egypt. This he did, leaving that very hour, and none too soon, for Herod sent his soldiers with the order to kill all the boys of two years and younger in the region of Bethlehem. The gifts of the Oriental wise men served to support the family while in Egypt, where they stayed until the death of the wicked king Herod. Then they returned to Nazareth.

When Jesus was twelve years old, Joseph and Mary took Him with them to the yearly Passover festival in Jerusalem. On their way home, they suddenly realized that the Boy was not with their company of travelers. They returned to Jerusalem and spent the next three days frantically searching for Him. At last they decided to look in the Temple, and there they heard His childish voice. He was "sitting with the Jewish teachers, listening to them and asking questions. All who heard him were amazed at his intelligent answers . . . His mother said to him, 'Son, why have you done this to us? Your father and I have been terribly worried trying to find you.'

"He answered them, 'Why did you have to look for me? Didn't you know that I had to be in my Father's House?' But they did not understand his answer."[8]

Jesus identified Himself with God, calling Him "FATHER," and the Temple He named as "God's House." Was Jesus inquiring of the priests about the significance of the sheep sacrifices which He had witnessed in the Temple? We do not know. He returned then to Nazareth with His parents.

Nothing more is known of the childhood and youth of Jesus who grew to manhood working in Joseph's carpenter shop in Nazareth. One short statement summarized this period of His life: "The child grew and became strong; he was full of wisdom, and God's blessings were upon Him."[9] We do know that His life from the beginning was empowered by the HOLY SPIRIT within Him, so that He lived a life totally without sin. No other man on earth has ever been able to do this.

At the age of thirty, Jesus left the carpenter's bench and went to Jerusalem. Shortly thereafter He was baptized in the Jordan River by His cousin John, who had become a famous preacher. Following the public baptism of Jesus, John announced, "There is the LAMB OF GOD WHO TAKES AWAY THE SIN OF THE WORLD.[10] Why did John call Jesus the "Lamb of God?" Why did he specify this animal used as a sacrifice in the temple services? We will soon understand.

Jesus now began His work which He had come into the world to do. Immediately the devil came to Him with a series of grueling temptations, far worse than the simple temptation which had led Adam and Eve to disobey God! Satan was very eager to overcome the SON of God in His vulnerable human form. But unlike Adam and Eve, Jesus overcame each test by relying upon the power which God gave Him. He did not separate Himself from God's ever-present help as they had. As a Man, He also understood, from His knowledge of the Hebrew Scriptures, the truth about the war between God and Lucifer (Satan, the devil).

Jesus chose twelve ordinary men of various ages and occupations to be His disciples. Several were fishermen, one was a tax collector. They were attracted by His righteous character, His forthright teachings and His mastery of every situation. Jesus had great compassion and as He passed from town to town, His fame as a great Healer preceded Him. Sick people with every kind of hopeless disease were brought to Him. By divine miracles, He immediately brought all back to complete health and soundness of body. Often after He had healed them, He said, "Your sins are forgiven. Go and sin no more." Many towns which Jesus visited had not one sick or disabled person remaining after He had passed through.

He taught about God's coming Kingdom by telling stories with deep meaning, drawing illustrations from current happenings or from nature. His work for others was tireless. Yet He had enemies— the priests and rulers of the Jews. "How can this unlearned carpenter forgive sins? By what authority does He teach the people, and especially forgive sins? Only God has the power and right to remove sin. How dare this mere man assume the authority that only God has!" So thought the priests who tried over and over to trap Him in a misstatement, an untruth, an inconsistency of life or teaching.

But always Jesus showed the utmost wisdom and insight in dealing with them. He did not hesitate to point out their errors in direct manner, which only further angered them.

On three occasions Jesus raised people from death to life again. One of those resurrected, a dear friend, had been dead and entombed for four days. Again the priests attempted to discredit these acts as mere magic, under the influence of the devil. In spite of the controversy with the religious leaders, Jesus was popular and greatly loved by the common people. Some of them were convinced that He must be the long-awaited SAVIOR—the SEED of the woman—sent from God. Jesus' public ministry lasted only three and a half years, being cut short when one of this own disciples betrayed Him.

The day of the great national yearly celebration, the Passover Feast, drew on. When twelve years old, Jesus had observed this event in Jerusalem with His parents. In commemoration of the Hebrews' deliverance from Egyptian slavery centuries before, the

109

Passover was still annually kept. This had been not only a historical escape from bondage, but was also to symbolize the eventual release of God's people from the captivity of Satan and sin.

Under the guidance of God and the leadership of Moses, each Hebrew family that first Passover evening in Egypt, had killed a lamb. They had been directed to wipe its blood over the doorways of their houses. This was a sign for God's destroying angel to PASS OVER their houses, when the firstborn of all the Egyptians were to be killed. The lamb's blood was a sign that the Hebrew firstborn were to be SAVED from death in that crisis hour. Moreover, the flesh of the roasted lamb was eaten, but no bones in its body were to be broken. This entire epic bore deep symbolic meaning.

Since that time the ceremony had been repeated each year with the sacrifice and eating of the PASS-OVER LAMB. It was being conducted yet in Jesus' day, in addition to the daily morning and evening lamb sacrifices in Jerusalem's Temple. Lambs and oxen had been sacrificed from the time of Adam at Eden's border gate, pointing forward to this very time! Even in China, a yearly "BORDER SACRI-FICE" was conducted, though its significance was no longer understood.

On the evening before the Passover, Thursday

night, Jesus called His twelve disciples together in the upper room of a house. While they all sat at a table, He "took a piece of bread, gave thanks to God, broke it, and said, 'THIS IS MY BODY, WHICH IS BROKEN FOR YOU.'"[11] Then each of the men ate portions of the bread. Eating of the Passover lamb had also symbolized the body of Jesus, which was soon to "be broken."

Next He passed around sweet wine for each to drink, saying, "THIS IS . . . MY BLOOD WHICH IS POURED OUT FOR MANY FOR THE FORGIVE-NESS OF SINS. I tell you, I will never again drink this wine until the day I drink the new wine with you in my Father's Kingdom."[12] But the disciples all failed to understand the deep significance of the service. Nor did they relate it to the Passover Lamb's blood which had been wiped over the doorposts in Egypt, thereby SAVING the firstborn.

After leaving the room that evening, Jesus and His friends, except for one who had excused himself early, went to a garden to pray. However, sleep overcame all of His followers, and Jesus alone prayed to the FATHER in Heaven for strength to go through the ordeal He faced ON BEHALF OF ALL MANKIND.

While Jesus was still there in the garden, a noisy crowd approached and from their midst the missing disciple stepped forth and kissed Him. At this signal, Jesus was arrested and taken prisoner. Suddenly He was alone in the hands of an angry mob, for His disciples had fled. Now read once more (pp. 98-100) the amazing details of the prophecy recorded over 500 years before of the events to occur this night. THE TIME HAD COME!

CHAPTER **11**

RESOLVING THE ALTAR
OF HEAVEN MYSTERY

It was before dawn on Friday morning. Jesus, with hands bound, was pushed and shoved through the dark and empty streets of Jerusalem toward the house of the high priest. But the high priest was not alone. A number of teachers of the law and other religious leaders had gathered in his home at this unusual hour. As an unofficial, assembled council, they attempted to find some crime of which to accuse Jesus so that they could demand His death.

Many false witnesses came forward with lying statements. These seemed insufficient until finally two men stepped up and said, "This man said, 'I am able to tear down God's Temple and three days later

113

build it back up.' "[1] Immediately the high priest demanded that Jesus reply to this accusation. When He remained silent, the high priest said to him, "I charge you under oath by the living God: Tell us if you are the Christ, the Son of God."

"Yes, it is as you say," Jesus replied. "But I say to all of you: In the future you will see the Son of Man sitting at the right hand of the Mighty One and coming on the clouds of heaven."[2]

In horror, the high priest tore his priestly garments and cried, "Blasphemy! This man claims to be God! You have just heard Him. What do you think?"

They all answered, "He is guilty and must die!" So they spat in His face, and slapped and beat Him. They put Him in chains and led Him off to the Roman governor, for the Jews could not, by themselves, effect His execution, since they were under the Roman rule.

Next, Pontius Pilate, the Roman governor questioned Him, "Are you the king of the Jews?" Jesus neither answered him, nor to the many accusations being made by the priests. Puzzled, the governor declined to make a decision, sending Him off instead to the local ruler over that region. Having heard much about Jesus, the ruler hoped to see Him perform some miracles. He asked Him many questions, but again Jesus remained silent. Because He did not respond to their purposeless inquiries, the ruler and his soldiers treated Him with contempt. In mockery, they put a fine purple robe, the color of royalty, on Him and sent Him back to the governor, Pilate.

Now Pilate could no longer postpone his decision. He said to the priests and Jewish leaders, "Neither the ruler nor I have found this man guilty of any crime worthy of death. I will have Him whipped and let Him go."[3] But the gathering crowd cried out, "Kill Him! "

Pilate wanted to set Jesus free, and since it was the custom at Passover time to free whatever prisoner the crowd demanded be released, he asked them, "Shall I set free this criminal, Barabbas, or Jesus?" The crowd, influenced by the priests, demanded that Barabbas be freed and Jesus be put to death. When Pilate realized that a riot might break out if he did not comply with the wishes of the people, he took some water and washed his hands before them saying, "I am not responsible for the death of this man. This is your doing! "[4]

So, through a great failure of justice, this noble Man, the SON OF GOD, was lashed by the Roman whips until His back was torn and bleeding; a crown of thorns was placed on His head in ridicule. Blows to the head drove the thorns into His brow, until the blood streamed down His face. He was spit upon, and then made to carry His own heavy wooden cross, for crucifixion was the method of execution used by the cruel Romans. The place of crucifixion was on a small hill, called Calvary. When Jesus stumbled under the load, weak from the torture and abuse which had been heaped upon Him, a stranger from a foreign country was made to carry the cross for Him.

Calvary was located OUTSIDE JERUSALEM'S GATE. How important this fact is, for the Hebrew Scriptures relate:

> So Jesus also suffered OUTSIDE THE GATE in order to sanctify the people through His own blood.[5]

Even as Adam's sacrifice of unblemished lambs had been OUTSIDE EDEN'S GATE, so also was the Lamb of God to be offered OUTSIDE of Jerusalem, the holy Hebrew city. This too was a fulfillment of the ancient Chinese BORDER SACRIFICE, the "Border" being Eden's gate, typifying Jerusalem's gate where the Great Sacrifice for all mankind was to be made.

Roman soldiers laid out Jesus on the cross, nailing His outstretched arms, as well as his feet, to the rough wooden cross beneath. They then unmercifully dropped the cross into a prepared hole in the ground, which caused the weight of His body to tear the flesh of His palms and feet into gaping wounds. He took all the abuse without an outcry, except to murmur, "Forgive them, Father! They don't know what they are doing."[6] The crosses of two thieves scheduled for execution at the same time stood on either side of the central cross where Jesus hung.

Let us make a mental picture of the scene. Three crosses are silhouetted on a hill against a darkening sky. On the highest central cross, hangs the SON OF GOD. As we see the SAVIOR *hanging with outstretched, upraised arms,* held fast by the cruel nails through His hands, we remember a familiar figure . How many times have we seen symbols of *ShangTi* STANDING ON THE MOUNTAIN WITH ARMS UPRAISED IN BLESSING: , ,  ? What greater blessing is there than the sacrifice Jesus was making at that hour for ALL MANKIND?

sacrifice

It was 9 a.m., the time of the morning *sacrifice*  (祀 , p. 85) of the lamb in the Temple, when Jesus was hung upon the cross. He suffered anguish from terrible physical pain. But worse still was the knowledge that the sins of all mankind which were put upon Him were crushing out His life and separating Him from God, the FATHER. He cried out, "My God, My God, why have you forsaken me?"[7]

As Jesus endured the pain and mockery of the cross, He died the sinners' death— that death which is a solitary one, without God, without hope of a resurrection to life again. Jesus was even willing to give up His life in heaven forever if it meant saving mankind from eternal death. He died for lost mankind of all generations—from Adam and Eve's time, and yes, into the future—to the end of time.

sacrificial
animals

It was 3 p.m., the hour of the evening *sacrifice* 犠 (犧 , p. 85), when Jesus spoke His Last words, "It is finished! "[8], and breathed His last. THE SACRIFICE OF THE AGES WAS COMPLETE! Every unblemished lamb or bull offered in the past had pointed forward to this very hour. IT WAS THE VERY MOMENT IN TIME, AND THE ACT WHICH HAD SO PUZZLED THE SAGE, CONFUCIUS! THE SACRIFICIAL DEATH OF JESUS HAD BEEN REPRESENTED BY THOUSANDS OF BURNING BULLS OFFERED BY SUCCESSIVE EMPERORS OF CHINA AT THE ANNUAL BORDER SACRI-FICE, AND EVEN IN OUR 20th CENTURY THIS ANCIENT RITE WAS STILL BEING CONDUCTED AT PEKING'S ALTAR OF HEAVEN!

The reigning Ruler of China at the time of Jesus' death was Emperor *Kuang Wu* 光武帝 .[9] Perhaps his name, "The Hero of Light" was also prophetic, for many thousands of miles away from China, unbeknown to the Chinese, the world's greatest Hero of all time had given His life for the world. Jesus had

118

never called Himself a "Hero," but He had said, "I am the LIGHT of the World. Whoever follows me will have the LIGHT OF LIFE, and will never walk in darkness."[10] One of His disciples later said of Him that He was "the TRUE LIGHT that comes into the world and shines on ALL MANKIND."[11]

A bold Roman soldier, not being certain whether Jesus had indeed died, thrust a spear into His side, and out flowed blood and water—the "Water of Life." His death, Jesus had promised would mean *ETERNAL* 衍 (B)[12] (永) LIFE for everyone who would believe that He truly was the SON OF GOD. How appropriate that the inventor of Chinese writing more than 2000 years before had written *eternal* 衍 to resemble the flowing water of the River of Life! Not only that, but look closely and you will see God (Jesus) as a *MAN* 彳 in the very center of 衍 , surrounded by an artistically arranged 氵 , indicating God's presence (compare 示 , pp. 56, 57).

eternal

彳 (彳)	+	氵 (氵)	=	衍
a Man (Jesus)		*God's presence*		*eternal*

There is another very clever ancient character picturing ETERNAL LIFE. It is beautifully inscribed in the Bronzeware depiction of *long life* 壽 (B)[13] (壽). This pictogram once again portrays *ShangTi*

long life

119

as the *central* 大 (方) Being, forming also the Holy Mountain ∧ (compare 䀻 , 䀻 p. 49). This time the three Persons of the Godhead are represented, not only by three pairs of upraised arms 手 , but also by the three *Mouths, Persons* ʊʊʊ (口) arranged along the curving line descending from the Sacred Mount as the River of Life 〈 . It was not only the SON OF GOD who suffered, but also the FATHER and the SPIRIT. This SACRIFICE was their precious gift to mankind:

> For God so loved the world that He GAVE his only SON that WHOEVER believes in him should not perish, but have ETERNAL LIFE.[14]

For Jesus' disciples, the darkest hour had come. They had built their hopes upon His becoming the King who would throw off the Roman rule. Even they did not then understand His true UNIVERSAL MISSION—on behalf of ALL MANKIND AROUND THE EARTH, and not for Judah alone.

Two wealthy, and heretofore secret friends and believers of Jesus, now came forward to claim His body. Not one bone of His body had been broken. If He had not died before sunset, the soldiers would have taken Him off the cross and broken His legs to hasten His death. Recall that no bones of the Passover lamb were to be broken. JESUS WAS THAT LAMB!

Those eminent men now wrapped His body in strips of cloth and placed Him in a new tomb, cut out of a rock, which had actually been purchased for one of them. A great stone was rolled before the opening. Roman guards posted at the request of the high priest, watched the tomb to prevent His disciples from stealing away the body. They remembered Jesus saying on a number of occasions that He would be resurrected on the third day: "Destroy this Temple [His body], and in three days I will raise it again."[15]

The weekly seventh day of REST, commemorating His original six days of work in creating the earth and all plant and animal life, was drawing on as the sun set in the western sky. This Sabbath, the world's Creator *RESTED*  (止) in the tomb. He had accomplished for mankind His appointed mission of making possible the RE-CREATION of man's character through His own gift of *righteousness* 公義. How significant that this ideographic combination conveys the idea that *righteousness* is open to *ALL* 公 MANKIND—all the descendants of Adam!

to rest

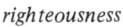
righteousness

all

> "For just as ALL people die because of their union with Adam, in the same way ALL will be raised to life because of their union with Christ" [Jesus] .[16]

Very early on the third day after His death, the first day of the week, there was an earthquake. An angel descended from heaven and rolled back the great stone from the mouth of the tomb. The guarding Roman soldiers dropped to the ground as dead men at the dazzling brightness of the angel. Jesus stepped forth from the tomb, the resurrected SAVIOR! The fallen "Temple of God" had indeed been restored in three days, according to His promise.

The risen SON OF GOD appeared to His disciples and to many others on several occasions. At last, forty days after His resurrection, He and His disciples walked past the garden where He had prayed the night of His arrest, and on to the Mount of Olives.

> When he had led them out to the vicinity of Bethany, he LIFTED UP HIS HANDS AND BLESSED THEM. While he was blessing them, he left them and was taken up into heaven.[17]

Our final picture of Jesus, the SON OF GOD, is of Him on the Mount of Olives, with UPRAISED ARMS IN BLESSING. It was the same posture that *ShangTi,* from the very beginning, had taken on the Holy Mount when Adam and Eve *returned* 反 (旋 , p. 49) there to worship.

to return

As His disciples watched, He began to rise from the earth, being transported by a host of joyous angels, one of whom announced: "THIS JESUS WHO

WAS TAKEN FROM YOU INTO HEAVEN, WILL COME BACK IN THE SAME WAY THAT YOU SAW HIM GO TO HEAVEN."[18] Heaven had promised something, still unfulfilled, which we, nearly two thousand years later, must seriously ponder. Does this sacred pledge still have meaning for me today?

CHAPTER **12**

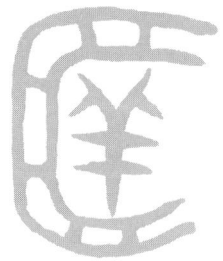

SHANGTI'S
LAST PROMISE

We began this little book with a question: "Where did I come from?" But there are equally puzzling questions frequently contemplated by most everyone: "Why am I here?" "Is there more to life than this?" "Will I live again after this life?" In other words, "Where am I going?"

Jesus, the SON OF GOD, said to His disciples while He was here on earth:

> "Do not be worried or upset. Believe in God, and believe also in me. There are many rooms in my Father's house, and I am going to prepare a place for you. I would not tell you this if it were not so. And after I go and prepare a place for you, I WILL COME BACK and take you to myself, so that you will be where I am

. . . NO ONE GOES TO THE FATHER EXCEPT BY ME."[1]

We can read more about the place where Jesus went, and is still living today, in the Holy Bible, which is *ShangTi's* own book. He has built a beautiful City in heaven, called the New Jerusalem. It has a great high wall with twelve pearly gates. The City is perfectly square. Its height is equal to its length and breadth because a magnificent mountain rises in its center. The wall is made of jasper and the City itself of pure gold, clear as glass. Twelve kinds of beautiful, shining jewels are set in the twelve foundations of the wall, giving it a rainbow effect. In this City, Jesus is called "the Lamb," because of His sacrifice for the human race. Those whose names are written in the "Lamb's Book of Life"—those who accept Jesus as their SAVIOR from sin—can enter the City.

In the middle of the City is *ShangTi's* throne on the majestic Mount Zion. From the throne flows the River of Life, and on either side of the River is the Tree of Life.[2] But wait a minute, was there not a Tree of Life in the Garden of Eden, man's first home on earth? In that Garden, in the very center, on a great mountain, were two special trees, the Tree of Life and the Tree of the Knowledge of Good and Evil. Flowing from the top of the mountain was a beautiful River which divided into four heads and became four Rivers.

The ancient symbol for *garden* ⊞ very accurately pictures the four Rivers arising from the center of the square Garden. In other words, THE GARDEN OF EDEN WAS A BEAUTIFUL EARTHLY MINIATURE REPLICA OF THE CITY OF *SHANGTI* IN HEAVEN. One ancient form of *garden* 𐤀 (U)[3] (田) depicts God Ψ in the very center of the *Garden* with arms upraised. The source of the Rivers was the "Fountain of Life," a unique symbolism for the source of all life in *ShangTi,* Himself.

garden

In the second and third chapters, *ShangTi* was identified as the Creator of heaven, earth, and all living things. This was shown by both the venerable Chinese BORDER SACRIFICE recitations (pp. 10 11, 19, 30), and the ancient pictographic Chinese characters. *ShangTi* created all things by calling them into existence (p. 19). Jesus is also identified as the Creator in the Hebrew scriptures, the Holy Bible, where He is called "the WORD," because He too SPOKE everything into existence:

> Before the world was created, the WORD already existed; He was with God, and He was the SAME AS GOD. From the very beginning the WORD was with God. THROUGH HIM, GOD MADE ALL THINGS; not one thing in all creation was made without Him. The WORD was the source of life, and this life brought light to

mankind . . . THE WORD WAS IN THE WORLD, and though GOD MADE THE WORLD THROUGH HIM, yet the world did not recognize Him. He came to His own country, but His own people did not receive Him. Some however, did receive Him and believed in Him, So He gave them the right to become God's children.[4]

Note that through the "WORD," Jesus, God made all things. Jesus, the SON, was the AGENT of *ShangTi* in His creative work. The SPIRIT was also an AGENT in creation. The three Persons of the Godhead worked as ONE in creating our world. From the Chinese pictograms, we might be inclined to give Jesus the name of *"Shen"* 示(⺊), 示⌇, 示⺈ (神), for this name reveals the very creative work of God in forming Adam (and Eve) with His own hands (pp. 23-25; 38).

Jesus, Himself, had declared, "The FATHER and I are ONE."[5] This is indeed a strange statement, and even his disciples did not immediately understand it. One disciple, Philip, asked, "Lord, show us the FATHER and we ask no more." To this Jesus replied:

"Anyone who has seen me has seen the Father . . . Do you not believe that I am in the Father, and the Father in me? I am not myself the source of the words I speak to you. It is the FATHER WHO DWELLS IN ME DOING HIS OWN WORK."[6]

128

This explains how the *FATHER* 𠂤 (父) is the Creator through the agency of the SON, *Shen.* So the symbols, 𠂤 (p. 30) are also thereby explained, where the *FATHER* 𠂤 appears to be creating Adam, the *adult male* ● , or Eve 𠂤 , the *second* (p. 36). How truly the Chinese writing and the Hebrew Scriptures agree!

The SPIRIT, as just mentioned, was also an agent in creation, and this activity too is explicitly seen in the character for *SPIRIT* 靈 (靈). Here the three *Persons* ∪∪∪ of the Godhead (the FATHER, SON and HOLY SPIRIT) are depicted. The *work* 工 of creating the first human couple, two *persons* ∤ ㇉ (∤㇉) is likewise portrayed (p. 56).

Therefore, we can say that although *ShangTi, Shen* and the SPIRIT are three separate Personalities, yet their purposes are ONE, and their work is ONE. The CHINESE TRINITY IS EXACTLY THE SAME AS THE HEBREW GODHEAD— THE ALL-POWER-FUL CREATOR, SUSTAINER AND SAVIOR OF THE EARTH; THE RULER OF THE ENTIRE UNIVERSE.

Is it any accident that when Jesus, the SON, gave His life as the *Lamb* 羔 of God in sacrifice for man's sins, that He was nailed to a cross—a *tree* 木 ? This ugly *tree* 木 of suffering has become the "Tree of Life" and immortality for all! In God's beautiful new City, there is no Tree of the Knowledge of Good and Evil, which formerly stood next to the Tree of Life in the center of the earthly Garden. There will be no temptation in the new Garden of Eden, the Holy City, for Satan (Lucifer, the devil, the old serpent) will have been forever destroyed.

Jesus has promised to return to our earth again. At that time, the earth will be destroyed by His glorious presence. Rebellious mankind has departed far from righteousness, and followed the devil's example instead. The result has been war, bloodshed, crime, unfaithfulness and misery. The devil has had his opportunity to demonstrate his kind of dominion and government on the earth. And now once more, *ShangTi* will put an end to the reign of sin on earth, as He did by the war in heaven (see pp. 63, 64).

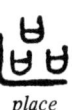

place

The second coming of Jesus will result in the "end of the world." How can one be saved from the destruction and death which will sweep over the entire earth on that day? The only safe hiding *place* 凷凷 (O)[7] (匽) will be in God's care. ⊏ (O)[8] (⊏) means *to conceal, hide,* and the three *persons* 凷凷 are identified as the TRINITY, the Godhead. This safe *place* 凷凷 of *hiding* ⊏ is ONLY with God. The end of all things is fast approaching.

to conceal, hide

While Jesus was on earth, His disciples came to Him with the question, "WHAT WILL BE THE SIGN

OF YOUR COMING AND OF THE END OF THE
WORLD?" So He gave them a list of events to look
for:

1. False Christs and false prophets will deceive many.
2. Wars and rumors of wars; nations rising against nations.
3. Earthquakes in increasing intensity and frequency.
4. Wickedness and crime will be multiplied.
5. Persecution of righteous people.
6. Famines and pestilence.
7. Life going on as usual; most people unaware of approaching doom because of unbelief in God.
8. The Good News of salvation through Jesus Christ will be brought to every nation, and then the end will come.[9]

No one need be ignorant of what is coming upon
the earth. The Bible is full of warnings. But we are
told that few will believe that Jesus is really coming
again, and SOON:

You must understand that IN THE LAST
DAYS some people ... will make fun of
you and will ask, "He promised to come,
didn't He? Where is He? Our fathers have
already died, but everything is still the
same as it was since the creation of the
world!" ... But the heavens and earth
that now exist are being preserved by the
same command of God, in order to be
destroyed by fire. They are being kept for
the day when godless people will be judged

and destroyed.[10]

But those faithful to God will be saved from this destruction, taken away from the earth before it is destroyed. They will be *delivered* 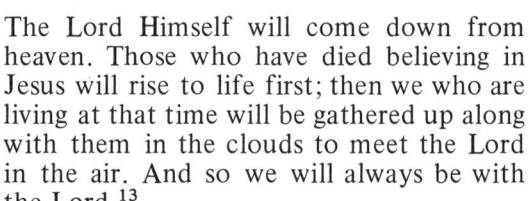$_{(O)}$[11] (匡), and by whom? The bronzeware writing of this character, $_{(B)}$[12], leaves no doubt that it is the *Lamb* (羊) who is the *Deliverer* and will *hide* His people in that day. It will happen like this:

to deliver

> The Lord Himself will come down from heaven. Those who have died believing in Jesus will rise to life first; then we who are living at that time will be gathered up along with them in the clouds to meet the Lord in the air. And so we will always be with the Lord.[13]

Here is the answer to the question concerning death which, you will remember, Confucius avoided answering (p. 9). It was evidently a mystery which he did not attempt to discuss. However, there is this promise of a RESURRECTION OF ALL THE FAITHFUL DEAD OF ALL AGES. Righteous man will live again! (p. 98). And we can know that God, the wise judge, will deal justly, taking into consideration the opportunities of each to learn and act upon truth as it comes to him.

Some will be fortunate in not having to taste death at all—"we who are living at that time." These faithful ones will be taken directly to heaven on that day when Jesus returns. And what of the earth?

> On that Day the heavens will disappear
> with a shrill noise, the heavenly bodies
> will burn up and be destroyed and the
> earth with everything in it will vanish.[14]

But there is a promise of a new earth after the destruction of the present one with the erradication of sin and sinners:

> "Then I saw a new heaven and a new earth.
> The first heaven and the first earth dis-
> appeared, and the sea vanished. And I saw
> the Holy City, the New Jerusalem, coming
> down out of heaven from God, prepared
> and ready, like a bride dressed to meet
> her husband. I heard a loud voice speaking
> from the throne: 'Now God's home is with
> mankind! He will live with them, and they
> shall be his people. God himself will be
> with them, and He will be their God. He
> will wipe away all tears from their eyes.
> There will be no more death, no more grief
> or crying or pain. The old things have
> disappeared."[15]

God will make His dwelling place with man on this earth which will then become the capital of the entire universe. His *Imperial Domain* 㽥 (B)[16] (甸), His throne, will be in their midst. How appropriate that again the miniature of God's beautiful City, the *Garden* 田 of Eden is seen in this character! Rising above all in this beautiful celestial Garden in the New Jerusalem, is God's lofty throne on Mount Zion.

Imperial Domain

... the River of the water of Life, sparkling like crystal, and coming from the throne of God and of the Lamb and flowing down the middle of the City's street. On each side of the River is the Tree of Life, which bears fruit twelve times a year, once each month ... The throne of God and of the Lamb will be in the City, and His servants will worship Him. THEY WILL SEE HIS FACE ... There will be no more night ... because the Lord God will be their light, and they will rule as kings forever and ever.[17]

The *Imperial Domain* 田 shows God's *Garden* 田 paradise and the great *Being* 〕 (入), God Himself.

This earth and its human inhabitants have, since creation, been the object of *ShangTi's* greatest love and concern. Very soon, the lengthy controversy between *ShangTi* and the devil will be over. The war has already been decided. But WE must choose to be on the right side—the winning side!

God gives the invitation to all:

"Come! Whoever is thirsty, accept the Water of Life as a gift, whoever wants it."[18]

barrier

There will be no more *barrier* (關) at the Garden *gate*. All who love and obey God may freely come and go into the new Garden of Eden on earth. No one will be excluded from the *Tree* 木 of Life. Everyone may eat the fruit which gives everlasting life. Best of all, we can all *meet* (見) face-

meet

to-face (p. 90) with *ShangTi,* as did Adam and Eve in the beginning.

> Happy are those who DO His command-
> ments and so have the RIGHT to eat the
> fruit from the Tree of Life and to go
> THROUGH the gates into the City.[19]

Let the ancient Chinese characters speak TRUTH to you! These must have been preserved in the earth for more than 4,000 years for our very day to convince us that *ShangTi* still lives! The great Sovereign of heaven, Creator of the earth, loves and has a vital interest in EACH INDIVIDUAL.

> For I am certain that nothing can separate
> us from his love: neither death nor life,
> neither angels nor other heavenly rulers or
> powers, neither the present nor the future,
> neither the world above nor the world
> below—there is nothing in all creation that
> will ever be able to separate us from the
> love of God which is ours through Christ
> Jesus our Lord."[20]

Now we can fully appreciate the Oracle Bone rendering of *Ti (ShangTi)!* In this ancient script, we find the ORIGINAL *RULER* of heaven and earth, Ti 帝(O)[21](帝), represented as the Trinity with three *MOUTHS, PERSONS* ▽ + ▷ + ◁ (compare ß, p. 54; 齋, p. 56).

It would appear that the lower part of this figure, ∧, represents a shortened form of a *tree* 木

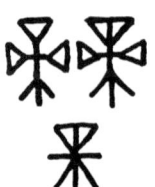

ShangTi

*Imperial
Sacrifice*

(actually the TREE OF LIFE, symbolic of eternal life which only *ShangTi* can bestow). In additional forms, 禾(O)[21], 禾(O)[22], the entire *tree* 木 is seen. Recall that we identified, earlier in the chapter (p. 129), the TREE OF LIFE with the CROSS, the "tree of suffering."

Yet another apparent "shorthand form" of *Ti*, the *RULER* is 禾(O)[21]. This figure is seen in the character for *IMPERIAL SACRIFICE* (BORDER SACRIFICE) 禘(O)[21] (禘), where the *hands* 𢍏 of the two worshipers are seen praising *Ti (ShangTi)* 禾. And so our Confucian riddles are completely solved!

But we know one more fact. This great loving *ShangTi* is still searching, yearning and pleading for lost mankind everywhere to return to Him:

"Turn to me now and be saved,
   people all over the world!
I AM THE ONLY GOD THERE IS.
My promise is true.
   and it will not be changed.
I solemnly promise by all that I am."[23]

136

A NEW LOOK
AT AN OLD LANGUAGE

When *Hsu Shen* compiled his time-honored *Shuo Wen* in 86 B.C., he not only set forth, to the best of his ability, the authentic character forms, but also made a first meager attempt to explain the derivation of many pictographic and ideographic characters from familiar objects of his day. THE *SHUO WEN* HAS BEEN THE BASIS FOR ANALYSIS OF CHINESE CHARACTERS SINCE THAT TIME, WITH MANY MORE RECENT SCHOLARS ADDING THEIR OWN IDEAS AS THE YEARS PASSED. But at least 2,000 years had elapsed in *Hsu Shen's* day since the invention of the writing, and today the venerable characters are more than

4,000 years old. Might there have been another, more methodical system, used by the ancient Chinese as the basis upon which to build their language, than everyday objects?

Ancient Egyptian scribes also had their own intricate pictographic writing, called hieroglyphs, meaning a "sacred writing." Built right into their script, were their peculiar religious concepts. We believe that the Chinese, too, may have created a hieroglyphic writing to preserve their sacred concepts, as our book has demonstrated. In other words, instead of a hit-or-miss calligraphy depicting only objects about them in their everyday life (which may have been very different from the world 2,000 or 4,000 years later), is it possible that the Chinese of antiquity had a real plan for their writing? This system might have been based upon their knowledge of the God, *ShangTi,* whom they worshiped at that time, and the relationship of God to the first human couple: namely, a record of the beginnings of human history and the interplay between God and man.

A brief, and of course, incomplete comparison between the existing method of character analysis and our "hieroglyphic" concept will be given to illustrate the plausibility of a systematic, graphic language which depicts actual sacred, historical narratives and facts.

First of all, we believe that God has, in the past, been little appreciated in the ancients' multiple artistic configurations depicting Him. These are important to recognize, and will therefore be cited:

1.   Pictograms (actually "stick figures" upon which we will append a "head") of God, ALWAYS WITH ARMS UPRAISED IN BLESSING, for example: ⊢ (" ⋔ ", p. 74); ⊢ (" ⋔ ", pp. 50, 82); Ψ (" Ψ ", pp. 21, 36, 37); ⋇ (" ⋇ ", pp. 38, 46, 51, 78); ⼤ (" ⼤ ", pp. 49, 120); ⋋ or ⊼ (pp. 28, 58); and ⼌ (pp. 30, 36, 37).

2.   Representations of God as a great *Person, Being* ⼎ (" ⼎ ", pp. 25, 38, 79, 119, 134); ⼍ (" ⼍ ", p. 66); ⼌ (" ⼌ ", pp. 30, 33, 36); ⼤ (" ⼤ ", p. 62); ⼍⼨ (p. 135). (Remember also that man was made in God's image, to look like Him), for example: ⼎ (pp. 43, 49, 51, 56, 62); ⼌ (" ⼌ ", p. 35); ⼤ (" ⼤ ", pp. 28, 29).

3.   A symbol of "God's presence," ≡ , meaning also breath (pp. 51-57). These three strokes (seen also as ⼁ p. 39, or ⼁⼁ p. 86), actually represent the three members of the Godhead, the Trinity.

4.   Use of the "God radicals," the most primitive being ⊤ or ⊤̄ (pp. 41, 46, 50, 57, 65, 83); also ⼍⼍ , ⼍⼍ , ⼍⼍ , ⼍⼍ pp. 57, 58, 61, 66, 83).

5.   Recognition of the creative Hand(s) of God ⟨⟩ ,

(} (p. 23, 24); ✔ (pp. 25, 35).

6.   Identification of God's earthly dwelling place—a Holy Mountain, for example: ⊓ (冇 , pp. 38, 49, 56); ⊃ (夛 , p. 50, 82); ∧ (乂 , p. 50, 70); 厂(⻛, p. 51); ⊨ , ⦃ , or ⦙ (pp. 51, 54, 92); etc.

Secondly, we must distinguish the first human couple, often conjoined (married) as more than just "two ordinary persons." In their sinless state they were sometimes decorated with a *flame of fire* • , symbolizing their reflection of God's glory. They may be identified, for example, as: *persons (mouths)* 🙂 , ⚬̥ , ⦃ (p. 38), ⩔ , ⌑ , ⦃ (pp. 39, 40), ⩔ (pp. 81, 82); having the second person emerging from the first as ⋏ (pp.47, 70, 78-82), ⓖ (p. 35), ◔ (p. 36); bowing figures ⅏ (" ⅂ + ⌐ ", pp. 37, 50), ⅂̧ (" ⟩ + ⌐", p. 62), ⟩⟩(" ⟩ + ⟩ ", pp. 49, 56); conjoined worshiping *hands* ⩞ (pp. 82, 83).

Thirdly, we may find in the characters various features of the Garden of Eden home of the first couple: the *Garden* ⊞ , 田 , 囶 (pp. 45, 67, 82, 83); the Holy Mountain (as above); a *Fountain* 爪 (p. 46); a holy *meeting* 名 (p. 90) *place* ⻛ (p. 50), 凷 (p. 130); a *river* ⫴ (pp. 50, 82, 119, 120); two special *trees* ⁑⁑ (pp. 65-68, 73); or the Garden *gate* ⊳⊲ , ⼧⼧ , ⼶⼶ (pp. 81, 83, 91).

It will become obvious why so many artistic variations for each of these depicted objects were necessary, as a single theme might be used repeatedly to express a great spectrum of appropriate meanings.

As illustrative samples are given to demonstrate the two theories of analysis, one can readily see that the *Shuo Wen* actually contains little analysis, and is in reality more of a dictionary. *Hsu Shen* had no access to either the Bronzeware or Oracle Bone writings. His recorded characters are all in the Seal writing. Consequently, he was disadvantaged in not being able to see the earliest forms. Therefore his comments prove really disappointing. Current analyses, of which there are many, now 4,000 years removed from their origins, will not be cited.

We will now discuss a number of characters describing the narrative of the two special trees in the Garden of Eden. This can be nicely arranged in chronological sequence. Our in-depth analyses, which may be reviewed, will be cited in parentheses. Alternate interpretations taken directly from the *Shuo Wen* will be found in quotation marks. Comparison of the two methods will give one the opportunity to decide if the ancient Chinese had a unique method of recording sacred, historical data.

BOTH *HSU SHEN* AND WE BELIEVE THAT THE CHARACTER 祇(神, p. 23), REFERS TO

GOD, THE CREATOR. *Hsu Shen* explains the meaning of this character with the phrase, "The God of Heaven 〔天神〕 leads out all creation."[1] He analyzes the character as being phonetic, composed of 示 and 申 , since the right hand radical, 申 , has the same sound, *shen,* as the entire character. He states that 示 , which we identify as the "God radical" (p. 57, 58), indicates "a revelation, auspicious or unlucky, from heaven. The two horizontal lines are the old form of 上 (上), [meaning *supreme, above*] ; and the 小 represents sun, moon and stars, or signs in heaven which reveal transcendant things to men."[2] *Hsu Shen does* not explain the right hand radical (丨) which is interpreted by us as God creating *man* 丨 by His *hands* (丿) (p. 23).

As anyone acquainted with Chinese characters will quickly recognize, we have given "ideographic" interpretation to many characters commonly classified as "phonetic." *Hsu Shen* originated this classification no doubt when he noted the phonetic similarity between a constituent radical and the character as a whole. Since he was unable to make ideographic sense from the character, he must have concluded that this "hodge-podge" of radicals was drawn together only because of similarity in sound.

We would like to emphasize once more, however, that there were remarkable "phonetic associations" in the spoken language between words long before writing was invented. Only a few of many recognized by the authors have been pointed out in the text (pp. 25, 46, 85).

Eight characters, all containing the common symbol, a *tree* 米 or *trees* 米米 will, of themselves, relate the dramatic story of how sin entered our world. These characters are: *to warn, refrain from* 米刂 (戒); *to restrict, prevent* 米土 (杜); *to travel* 米㫋 (招); *to stop, rest* 亻米 (休); *to covet, desire* 米欠米 婪); *sorrow* 米口米, 慜 (楚); *barrier, fence* 阝米刂 (閑); and *trouble, worry* 囗米 (困).

Since *Hsu Shen* analyzed the Seal characters of a much later vintage than the Oracle Bone rendition, his analysis of *to warn, refrain from* 米刂 (戒), does not seem to even fit. He indicates that the character "to warn is composed of joined hands 廾 and a spear 戈 , meaning to take a spear to warn someone not to approach."[3] There is little attempt in the *Shuo Wen* to analyze it. Our dissection (p. 65) follows the simple narrative where *God* 丁 warns *Adam* not to take (with the *hand* 刂) from the forbidden *tree* 米 .

This warning of *restriction* 米土 (杜) was given to Adam (p. 65), the man of *dust* 土 . According to *Hsu Shen,* the character merely indicates a "sweet crab apple"[4] and the *dust* 土 (土) radical is only phonetic.

Adam and Eve 呂 (p. 49) probably *traveled* 㭊 (梠) daily to the *tree* 木 to partake of the fruit giving immortality. Quoting *Hsu Shen,* " 梠 means the lintel of a door; 呂 is the phonetic."[5] Another analyst defines the character as "traveling," but gives no reason.

The character to *stop, rest* 休 (休) can represent Eve, the *person* 亻 who *stopped,* alone, at the forbidden *tree* 木 (p. 67). *Hsu Shen* merely says the word means "to stop and rest,"[6] whereas a second scholar warns "one must not stop under a tall tree and think."[6] This particular tree mentioned, 喬 , is not a fruit tree, but one used for making furniture.

Hsu Shen states regarding 婪 (婪) that it means "to covet or be greedy and is composed of 林 and 女 , being phonetic with 林 ."[7] We believe that the *woman* 女 (女) represents Eve who was the first person to *covet* anything. She *coveted* the fruit from the forbidden *tree* 木 (木) which stood next to the *Tree* 木 of Life (p. 68).

Sorrow 楚 (楚 , p. 73), *Hsu Shen* explains simply as "a shrub or kind of bramble and is composed of 林 and 疋 being phonetic with 疋 ."[8] In the ancient form 楚 , we can clearly see a *person* ○ *stopped* 止 (止) and eating (with the *mouth* ○). A second ancient form 楚 actually depicts Eve picking fruit from the forbidden *tree.* This act of disobedience brought *sorrow* to all mankind.

It was necessary for God to set up a *barrier* 卜¥⳪ (閑) at the *gate* 卜 ⳪ from which the disobedient couple had been expelled. They could no longer eat of the *Tree* 朿 (木) of Life or have immortality (p. 81). *Hsu Shen* merely defines this character as a "fence"[9] and does not try to give a reason for these radicals being brought together.

To worry 㘙 (困 , p. 73), deciphered by *Hsu Shen,* becomes "an old thatched house"[10] which is a far cry from the real reason for the first couple's worry. A second Oracle Bone rendition of this character, 朿 gives the reason for the trouble—it was because Eve *stopped* 屮 at the *tree* 人 (abbreviated).

This calligraphic series demonstrates how easy it is to follow a whole story by various pictographic characters.

The solution to the sin problem brought about by eating of the forbidden *tree* 朿 , is found in the *sheep* 全 (羊) and *bull* 屮 (牛) sacrifices which represented the vicarious death of the SAVIOR, God's SON, one member of the Godhead. In four characters featuring the *sheep* 羊 , we see this plan of salvation explained: *sacrificial animals* 犠 (犠); *righteous* 簛 (義); *beautiful* 黍 (美); and *to deliver*

匡 (匡).

For 犧, *Hsu Shen* records, "sacrificial animals for the temple, composed of 羊 and 牛, and being phonetic with 羲."[11] We agree that this character names the *sacrificial animals,* but we believe that these sacrifices were initiated at the Garden of Eden and were again symbolic and prophetic of the sacrifice of God's only Son. *Bull* 牛 and *sheep* 羊 sacrifices were also used by the Hebrews in their sacrifices to the God of Heaven, even as the Chinese did in their BORDER SACRIFICES to *ShangTi* (pp. 84).

Righteous 義, *Hsu Shen* explains as "righteousness in my appearance, being composed of [*I, me, my*] 我 and [*sheep*] 羊."[12] In our analysis, we indicate more fully the significance of this beautiful character. *I* 我 am made *righteous* 義 by the death of the *Lamb* 羊 of God (p. 79).

The character *beautiful* 美, is explained by *Hsu Shen* as "sweet, delicious, being composed of 羊 and 大"[13] More interesting is that he says "of the six livestock animals used for food, the sheep is the most important."[13] We believe that the sheep was the most important animal because of its symbolic representation of God's Son, the *Lamb* of God, whose sacrificial death would make us *beautiful* 美 in God's eyes. Therefore, we analyze 美 as a *sheep* 羊 covering a *noble man* 大, originally, Adam. God would see only

His sinless Son when looking upon the sinner thus covered by the Lamb (p. 80).

Lastly, we find the *sheep* 𦍌 once more featured in 匲 (匚), meaning, appropriately, *to deliver,* for it is the *Lamb* of God only who can *deliver* all from sin (p. 132). This character's analysis in the *Shuo Wen* of a "rice container," [14] again demonstrates the disadvantage of *Hsu Shen* in not having the Bronzeware character to examine.

Only a brief comparison of the two methods of analysis has been presented. It will be obvious to the reader that *Hsu Shen,* for the most part, defined the meaning of characters and did very little interpretation. He certainly did not attempt to discover why the characters were composed of different radicals as we have done. In his time, besides having no access to the most ancient characters, he knew nothing of the historical records of mankind's origin, namely the Hebrew writings as contained in the *Bible.* We are now fortunate to be able to examine these for similarities with the ancient Chinese ideographic characters.

Perhaps the above gives some insight into the logical system of "hieroglyphic," or "hierographic," writing, built upon the ancients' knowledge of their world and the loving relationship between early mankind and their Creator-God, *ShangTi.* How wonderful that we, 4,000 years later, can glimpse this primeval earth through the medium of well-stored pictures and ideas!

REFERENCES

CHAPTER 1: THE RIDDLE

1. James Legge, *The Chinese Classics (Vol iii), The Shoo King: Canon of Shun* (Taipei: Southern Materials Center Inc., 1932) pp. 33, 34.
2. James Legge, *The Notions of the Chinese Concerning God and Spirits* (Hong Kong: Hong Kong Register Office, 1852) pp. 24, 25.
3. Legge, op. cit., p. 30.
4. Legge, p. 31.

CHAPTER 2: WHO IS SHANGTI?

1. James Legge, *The Notions of the Chinese Concerning God and Spirits* (Hong Kong: Hong Kong Register Office, 1852) p. 28.
2. Legge, p. 29.
3. Legge, p. 29.
4. Legge, p. 30.
5. Legge, pp. 50, 51.
6. Lung Ch'uan Kwei T'ai Lang, *Shih Chi Hui Chu K'ao Cheng* (Taipei: Han Ching Wen Hua Enterprise Co. Ltd., 1983) p. 496.
7. Hsin Cheng Yu, *Ancient Chinese History*

(Taipei: Taiwan Commercial Press, 1963) p. 6.

8. Bradley Smith and Wan-go Weng, *China, A History in Art* (New York: Doubleday, 1972) p. 33.

9. G.D. Wilder and J.H. Ingram, *Analysis of Chinese Characters* (Taipei: Chin Wen Publ. Co., 1964) pp. iv-vi.

10. Genesis 1: 1, 2, 9, 10, 16, 27, 28, KJV.

CHAPTER 3: CHINESE CONCEPTS OF
EARTH'S BEGINNINGS

1. James Legge, *The Notions of the Chinese Concerning God and Spirits* (Hong Kong: Hong Kong Register Office, 1852) p. 29.

2. Psalm 33: 6, 9, TEV.

3. Genesis 1.

4. Genesis 1: 24, RSV.

5. Hung Pei Chiang, *Chih Ku Lu Chuan Wen* (Taipei: Lo Tien Publ. Co., 1974) Vol. ii, p. 1169.

6. Op. cit. p. 1341.

7. Op. cit. p. 1251.

8. Lin Chih Ch'ing, *Ting Cheng Liu Shu T'ung* (Shanghai: Kuang-I Publ. Co., 1936) part ii, p. 12.

9. Hung Pei Chiang, Vol. i, p. 351.

10. Op. cit. Vol. ii, p. 949.

11. Op. cit. Vol. ii, p. 1034.

12. Op. cit. Vol. ii, p. 1198.

13. Genesis 2: 7, KJV.

14. Chou Fa Kao, et al, *Ching Wen Ku Lin* (Hong Kong: Chinese University, 1975) p. 5198.

15. Hung Pei Chiang, Vol. i, p. 731.

16. Ma Wei Ching, *Wei Ching Chia Ku Wen Yuan* (Yunlin: Ma Fu Distributor, 1971) p. 511.

17. Hung Pei Chiang, Vol. 11, p. 1241.

18. Op. cit. p. 1270.

19. Genesis 1: 26, TEV.

20. Psalm 84: 11, KJV.

21. Hebrews 12: 29, KJV.

22. Hung Pei Chiang, Vol. ii, p. 1341.

23. Psalm 104: 1, 2, TEV.

24. Hung Pei Chiang, Vol. ii, p. 1302.

25. Genesis 1: 26, TEV.

26. Lung Ch'uan Kwei T'ai Lang, *Shih Chi Hui Chu K'ao Cheng* (Taipei: Han Ching Wen Hua Enterprise Co. Ltd., 1983) p. 497.

27. Hung Pei Chiang, Vol. ii, p. 1010.

28. Genesis 2: 25, NIV.

29. Hung Pei Chiang, Vol. ii, p. 1162.

30. Psalm 8: 5, NIV.

31. Chou Fa Kao, p. 5526.

32. Hung Pei Chiang, Vol. i, p. 49.

33. Legge, p. 29.

34. Hung Pei Chiang, Vol. i, p. 50.

35. Op. cit., Vol. ii, p. 1158.

36. Legge, p. 29.

37. Isaiah 64: 8, NIV.

38. Genesis 2: 19, 20, TEV.

39. Genesis 2: 18, TEV.

40. Chou Fa Kao, p. 6776.

CHAPTER 4: THE RIB STORY

1. Hung Pei Chiang, *Chih Ku Lu Chuan Wen* (Taipei: Lo Tien Publ. Co. 1974) Vol. ii, p. 1305.

2. Op. cit., p. 1014.

3. Genesis 2: 18, 21, 22, TEV.

4. Ma Wei Ching, *Wei Ching Chia Ku Wen Yuan* (Yunlin: Ma Fu Distributor, 1971) p. 39.

5. Lin Chih Ch'ing, *Ting Cheng Liu Shu T'ung* (Shanghai: Kuang-I Publ. 1936) part viii, p. 33 under 肊.

6. Genesis 2: 23, TEV.

7. Hung Pei Chiang, Vol. ii, p. 1012.

8. Op. cit. p. 1115.

9. Genesis 1: 28, RSV.

10. Hung Pei Chiang, Vol. ii, 757.

11. Op. cit., Vol. i, p. 183.

12. Chou Fa Kao, p. 5699.

13. Hung Pei Chiang, Vol. ii, p. 1251.

14. Ma Wei Ching, p. 675.

15. Hung Pei Chiang, Vol. ii, p. 803.

16. Op. cit., p. 1176.

17. Lin Chih Ch'ing, part iv, p. 20 under 能 .

18. Lin Chih Ch'ing, part ii, p. 12.

19. Chou Fa Kao, p. 8354.

20. Hung Pei Chiang, Vol. ii, p. 940.

21. Op. cit., p. 809.

22. Chou Fa Kao, p. 4775.

23. Ma Wei Ching, p. 1184.

24. Genesis 2: 24, NIV.

25. Lin Chih Ch'ing, part i, p. 9.

26. Hung Pei Chiang, Vol. ii, p. 1173.

27. Genesis 2:1-3, NIV.

28. Ma Wei Ching, p. 1340.

29. Lin Chih Ch'ing, part viii, p. 21.

30. Li Hsiao Ting, *Chia Ku Wen Tzu Chi Shih* (Thesis No. 50, Chung Yang Yen Chiu Yuan Li Shih Yan Yu Yan Chiu So, 1965) p. 447.

31. Ma Wei Ching, p. 1025.

CHAPTER 5: SECRETS OF A LOST GARDEN

1. Chou Fa Kao, et al, *Ching Wen Ku Lin* (Hong Kong: Chinese University, 1975) p. 12.

References

2. Op. cit., p. 13.

3. Ma Wei Ching, *Wei Ching Chia Ku Wen Yuan* (Yunlin: Ma Fu Distributor, 1971) p. 95.

4. Op. cit., p. 96.

5. Genesis 3: 20, KJV.

6. Ma Wei Ching, p. 783.

7. Hung Pei Chiang, *Ching Wen P'ien Ching Wen* (Taipei: Kung I Publ. Co., 1974) p. 373.

8. Op. cit., p. 670.

9. Genesis 2: 8-10, RSV.

10. Hung Pei Chiang, Vol. ii, p. 1233.

11. Lin Chih Ch'ing, *Ting Cheng Liu Shu T'ung* (Shanghai: Kuang-I Publ. 1936) Section 2, part iii, p. 2.

12. Ma Wei Ching, p. 57.

13. Op. cit., p. 1019.

14. Lin Chih Ch'ing, part iii, p. 11.

15. Psalm 36: 6-9, NKJV.

16. Genesis 2: 9, NIV.

17. Hung Pei Chiang, Vol. ii, p. 1302.

18. Hung Pei Chiang, Vol. ii, p. 1315.

19. Chou Fa Kao, p. 4235.

20. Hung Pei Chiang, *Ching Wen P'ien Ching Wen* (Taipei: Kung I Publ. Co. 1974) p. 347.

21. Ma Wei Ching, p. 898.

22. Hung Pei Chiang, op. cit., p. 350.

23. Ma Wei Ching, p. 675.

24. Chou Fa Kao, p. 5322.
25. Hung Pei Chiang, *Chih Ku Lu Chuan Wen,* (Taipei: Lo Tien Publ. Co. 1974), Vol. ii, p. 1034.
26. Ma Wei Ching, p. 117.
27. Op. cit. p. 116.
28. Psalm 24: 3-5, RSV.

CHAPTER 6: MORE ON THE NATURE OF *SHANGTI*

1. Chou Fa Kao, et al, *Ching Wen Ku Lin* (Hong Kong: Chinese University, 1975) p. 5699.
2. Ma Wei Ching, *Wei Ching Chia Ku Wen Yuan* (Yunlin: Ma Fu Distributor, 1971) p. 81.
3. Chou Fa Kao, p. 5699.
4. Ma Wei Ching, p. 81.
5. Op. cit., p. 70.
6. Op. cit., p. 70.
7. Op. cit., p. 70.
8. Op. cit., p. 42.
9. Hung Pei Chiang, *Chih Ku Lu Chuan Wen* (Taipei: Lo Tien Publ. Co. 1974) Vol. ii, p. 878.
10. Op. cit., p. 853.
11. Op. cit., p. 1044.
12. Genesis 1: 1, 2, KJV.
13. Psalm 104: 29, 30, NIV.
14. Genesis 2: 7, TEV.

15. Lin Chih Ch'ing, *Ting Cheng Liu Shu T'ung* (Shanghai: Kuang-I Publ. 1936) part iv, p. 24.

16. Hung Pei Chiang, *Ching Wen P'ien Ching Wen* (Taipei: Kung I Publ. Co., 1974) p. 280.

17. Chou Fa Kao, p. 290.

18. Ma Wei Chin, p. 1308.

19. Hung Pei Chiang, p. 54.

20. Ma Wei Ching, p. 95.

21. Op. cit., p. 1019.

22. Lin Chih Ch'ing, part ii, p. 12.

23. Hung Pei Chiang, *Chih Ku Lu Chuan Wen,* Vol. ii, p. 841.

24. Chou Fa Kao, p. 4547.

25. Lin Chih Ch'ing, part iii, p. 30.

CHAPTER 7: THE LETHAL BITE

1. Chou Fa Kao, et al, *Ching Wen Ku Lin* (Hong Kong: Chinese University, 1975) p. 86.

2. Ma Wei Ching, *Wei Ching Chia Ku Wen Yuan* (Yunlin: Ma Fu Distributor, 1971) p. 444.

3. Op. cit., p. 1390.

4. Ezekiel 28: 12-17, NIV.

5. Isaiah 14: 7-9, NIV.

6. Revelation 12: 7-9, RSV.

7. Ma Wei Ching, p. 1038.

8. Genesis 2: 16-18, NIV.

9. Hung Pei Chiang, *Chih Ku Lu Chuan Wen* (Taipei: Lo Tien Publ. Co. 1974) Vol. ii, p. 1082.

10. Lin Chih Ch'ing, *Ting Cheng Liu Shu T'ung* (Shanghai: Kuang-I Publ. 1936) part viii, p. 34.

11. Hung Pei Chiang, Vol. ii, p. 834.

12. Op. cit., p. 959.

13. Op. cit., p. 890.

14. Ma Wei Ching, p. 501.

15. Op. cit., p. 485.

16. Hung Pei Chiang, Vol. ii, p. 967.

17. Genesis 3: 1, TEV.

18. Genesis 3: 3, TEV.

19. Genesis 3: 4, 5, NIV.

20. Ma Wei Ching, p. 544.

21. Op. cit., p. 529.

22. Genesis 3: 6, RSV.

23. Hung Pei Chiang, *Ching Wen P'ien Ching Wen* (Taipei: Kung I Publ. Co., 1974) p. 659.

24. Lin Chih Ch'ing, Section 2, part v, p. 2.

25. Genesis 3: 6, RSV.

26. Genesis 3: 7, RSV.

27. Genesis 3: 7, RSV.

28. Ma Wei Ching, p. 1055.

29. Lin Chih Ch'ing, part i, p. 24.

30. Op. cit., part vi, p. 14 under 果 .

31. Hung Pei Chiang, *Chih Ku Lu Chuan Wen,*

Vol. ii, p. 916.

32. Genesis 3: 11, TEV.

33. Genesis 3: 12, 13, TEV.

34. Hung Pei Chiang, Vol. ii, p. 967.

35. Genesis 3: 15, NKJV.

36. Genesis 3: 16, NKJV.

37. Ma Wei Ching, p. 130.

38. Hung Pei Chiang, Vol. ii, p. 906.

39. Genesis 3: 17-19, NIV.

40. Ma Wei Ching, p. 1232.

41. Op. cit., p. 794.

42. Op. cit., p. 1239.

43. Genesis 3: 19, NIV.

CHAPTER 8: A COSTLY RESCUE PLAN

1. Genesis 3: 21, NIV.

2. Ma Wei Ching, *Wei Ching Chia Ku Wen Yuan* (Yunlin: Ma Fu Distributor, 1971) p. 1063.

3. Op. cit., p. 1061.

4. Op. cit., p. 1060.

5. Op. cit., p. 1106.

6. Hung Pei Chiang, *Chih Ku Lu Chuan Wen* (Taipei: Lo Tien Publ. Co., 1974) Vol. ii, pp. 1280, 1169.

7. John 1: 29, TEV.

8. Chou Fa Kao, et al. *Ching Wen Ku Lin* (Hong

Kong: Chinese University, 1975) p. 7047.

9. Ma Wei Ching, p. 454.

10. Op. cit., p. 455.

11. Genesis 3: 22-24, NIV.

12. Kung Kuang Lang, *P'ing An Wu P'u* (Taipei: Decision Magazine, December, 1985) p. 15.

13. Ma Wei Ching, p. 1230.

14. Chou Fa Kao, p. 6566.

15. Lin Chih Ch'ing, *Ting Cheng Liu Shu T'ung* (Shanghai: Kuang-I Publ., 1936) Part ii, p. 23.

16. Ma Wei Ching, p. 889.

17. Lin Chih Ch'ing, part viii, p. 11.

18. Op. cit., part ii, p. 34.

19. Ma Wei Ching, p. 469.

20. Hung Pei Chiang, Vol. ii, p. 1102.

21. Op. cit., p. 871.

22. Ma Wei Ching, p. 1231.

23. Chou Fa Kao, p. 2406.

24. Ma Wei Ching, p. 1023.

25. Op. cit., p. 1023.

26. Lin Chih Ch'ing, part v, p. 10.

27. Ma Wei Ching, p. 1028.

28. Op. cit., pp. 1029, 1027.

29. Lin Chih Ch'ing, part 1, p. 23.

30. Leviticus 9: 2, RSV.

31. Exodus 29: 39, RSV.

32. Genesis 4: 2-5, NIV.

33. Ma Wei Ching, p. 504.

34. Genesis 4: 15, RSV.

35. Genesis 4: 16, NIV.

CHAPTER 9: UNRAVELING A CONFUCIAN
PUZZLE

1. Genesis 3: 24, RSV.

2. Ma Wei Ching, *Wei Ching Chia Ku Wen Yuan* (Yunlin: Ma Fu Distributor, 1971) p. 707.

3. Op. cit., p. 692.

4. Zechariah 2: 8, RSV.

5. Li Hsiao Ting, *Chia Ku Wen Tzu Chi Shih* (Thesis No. 50, Chung Yang Yen Chiu Yuan Li Shih Yan Yu Yan Chiu So, 1965) p. 3235.

6. Op. cit., p. 3235.

7. Chou Fa Kao, et al, *Ching Wen Ku Lin* (Hong Kong; Chinese University, 1975) p. 6568.

8. Lin Chih Ch'ing, part ii, p. 30.

9. Op. cit., part v, p. 31.

10. Op. cit., part vii, p. 31 under 介 .

11. Op. cit. part vii, p. 15.

12. Isaiah 65: 25, RSV.

13. Psalm 51: 17, NIV.

14. James Legge, *The Chinese Classics (Vol. i) Confucian Analects* (Taipei: Southern Materials Center Inc., 1983) pp. 146, 147.

15. Op. cit., p. 206.

16. Op. cit., p. 202.

17. Op. cit., p. 202.

18. Op. cit., *Doctrine of the Mean,* p. 404.

19. Psalm 104: 29, 30, NIV.

20. Psalm 146: 4, RSV.

21. Daniel 12: 2, 3. RSV.

22. Isaiah 53, TEV.

23. R.H. Mathews, *Chinese-English Dictionary* (Cambridge, Ma.: Harvard University Press, thirteenth printing, 1975) p. 1167.

CHAPTER 10: THE SEED OF THE WOMAN

1. Luke 30-33, TEV.

2. Luke 1: 34, 35, TEV.

3. Luke 1: 38, TEV.

4. Matthew 1: 20, 21, TEV.

5. Luke 2: 10-12, TEV.

6. Micah 5: 2, 4, 5, TEV.

7. Matthew 2: 8, TEV.

8. Luke 2: 46-50, TEV.

9. Luke 2: 40, TEV.

10. John 1: 29, TEV.

11. 1 Corinthians 11: 23, 24, TEV.

12. Matthew 26: 28, 29, TEV.

CHAPTER 11: RESOLVING THE ALTAR OF HEAVEN MYSTERY

1. Matthew 26: 61, TEV.
2. Matthew 26: 63, 64, NIV.
3. Luke 23: 15, 16, TEV.
4. Matthew 27: 24, TEV.
5. Hebrews 13: 12, RSV.
6. Luke 23: 34, TEV.
7. Mark 15: 34, RSV.
8. John 19: 30, KJV.
9. R.F. Mathews, *Chinese-English Dictionary* (Cambridge, Ma.: Harvard University Press, thirteenth printing, 1975) p. 1167.
10. John 8: 12, TEV.
11. John 1: 9, TEV.
12. Hung Pei Chiang, *Chih Ku Lu Chuan Wen* (Taipei: Lo Tien Publ. Co., 1974) Vol. ii, p. 1281
13. Op. cit., p. 853.
14. John 3: 16, RSV.
15. John 2: 19, NIV.
16. 1 Corinthians 15: 22, TEV.
17. Luke 24: 50, 51, NIV.
18. Acts 1: 11, TEV.

CHAPTER 12: *SHANGTI'S* LAST PROMISE

1. John 14: 1-3, 6, TEV.
2. Revelation 1 and 2.
3. Lin Chih Ch'ing, *Ting Cheng Liu Shu T'ung* (Shanghai: Kuang-I Publ., 1936) Section 2, part iii, p. 2.
4. John 4: 1-4, 10-12, TEV.
5. John 10: 30, TEV.
6. John 14: 8-10, NIV.
7. Ma Wei Ching, *Wei Ching Chia Ku Wen Yuan* (Yunlin: Ma Fu Distributor, 1971) p. 755.
8. Op. cit., p. 1044.
9. Matthew 24.
10. 2 Peter 3, 4, 7, TEV.
11. Ma Wei Ching, p. 1283.
12. Hung Pei Chiang, *Chih Ku Lu Chuan Wen* (Taipei: Lo Tien Publ. Co., 1974) Vol. ii, p. 1032.
13. 1 Thessalonians 4: 16, 17, TEV.
14. 2 Peter 3: 10, TEV.
15. Revelation 21: 1-4, TEV.
16. Chou Fa Kao, et al, *Ching Wen Ku Lin* (Hong Kong: Chinese University, 1975) p. 7497.
17. Revelation 22: 1-5, TEV.
18. Revelation 22: 18, TEV.
19. Revelation 22: 14, NKJV.

20.   Romans 8: 38, 39, NIV.

21.   Ma Wei Ching, p. 183.

22.   Ma Wei Ching, p. 180.

23.   Isaiah 45: 22, 23, TEV.

EPILOG: A NEW LOOK AT AN OLD LANGUAGE

1.   Hsu Shen, *Shuo Wen* (Taipei: Li Ming Cultural Enterprises Ltd., 1980) p. 3.

2.   Op. cit., p. 2.

3.   Op. cit., p. 105.

4.   Op. cit., p. 242.

5.   Op. cit., p. 258.

6.   Op. cit., p. 272.

7.   Op. cit., p. 630.

8.   Op. cit., p. 274.

9.   Op. cit., p. 595.

10.   Op. cit., p. 281.

11.   Op. cit., p. 53.

12.   Op. cit., p. 639.

13.   Op. cit., p. 148.

14.   Op. cit., p. 642.

BIBLIOGRAPHY

Chou Fa Kao, et al, *Ching Wen Ku Lin*. Hong Kong: Chinese University, 1975.

Good News Bible: Today's English Version. New York: American Bible Society, 1976.

Holy Bible: King James Version. London: Collins' Clear-Type Press, 1967.

Holy Bible: New International Version. Grand Rapids: Zondervan Corporation, 1978.

Holy Bible: New King James Version. Nashville: Thomas Nelson, Inc., 1982.

Holy Bible: Revised Standard Version. Camden, N.J.: Thomas Nelson and Sons, 1952.

Hsin Cheng Yu, *Ancient Chinese History*. Taipei: Taiwan Commercial Press, 1963.

Hsu Shen, *Shuo Wen*. Taipei: Li Ming Cultural Enterprises Ltd., 1980.

Hung Pei Chiang, *Chih Ku Lu Chuan Wen,* Vol. I & II. Taipei: Lo Tien Publ. Co., 1974.

Hung Pei Chiang, *Ching Wen P'ien Ching Wen.* Taipei: Kung I Publ. Co., 1974.

Kang, C.H. and Nelson, Ethel R. *The Discovery of Genesis*. St. Louis: Concordia Publishing House, 1979.

Kung Kuang Lang, *P'ing An Wu P'u*. Taipei: Decision Magazine, December, 1985.

Bibliography

Legge, James, *The Chinese Classics (Vol. III), The Shoo King: Canon of Shun.* Taipei: Southern Materials Center Inc., 1932.

Legge, James, *The Chinese Classics (Vol. I), The Doctrine of the Mean.* Taipei: Southern Materials Center Inc., 1932.

Legge, James, *The Chinese Classics (Vol. I), Confucian Analects.* Taipei: Southern Materials Center Inc., 1932.

Legge, James, *The Notions of the Chinese Concerning God and Spirits.* Hong Kong: Hong Kong Register Office, 1852.

Li Hsiao Ting, *Chia Ku Wen Tzu Chi Shih.* Thesis No. 50, Chung Yang Yen Chiu Yuan Li Shih Yan Yu Yan Chiu So, 1965.

Lin Chih Ch'ing, *Ting Cheng Liu Shu T'ung.* Shanghai: Kuang-I Publ. Co., 1936.

Lung Ch'uan Kwei T'ai Lang, *Shih Chi Hui Chu K'ao Cheng.* Taipei: Han Ching Wen Hua Enterprise Co. Ltd., 1983.

Mathews, R.H., *Chinese-English Dictionary.* Cambridge, Ma.: Harvard University Press, thirteenth edition, 1975.

Ma Wei Ching, *Wei Ching Chia Ku Wen Yuan.* Yunlin: Ma Fu Distributor, 1971.

Smith, Bradley and Weng, Wan-go, *China. A History in Art.* New York: Doubleday, 1972.

Wilder, G.D., and Ingram, J.H., *Analysis of Chinese Characters.* Taipei: Chin Wen Publ. Co., 1964.

166

CHARACTER INDEX

Character Index

INDEX

Index

Send to: **READ BOOKS PUBLISHER**
P.O. BOX 776
S. LANCASTER, MA., 01561

I would like _____ additional copies of **MYSTERIES
CONFUCIUS COULDN'T SOLVE** ($6.95).

Name _____

Address _____

City/State/Zip _____

(Please add $1.50 postage and handling for one book, 50¢
for each additional book TO THE SAME ADDRESS.
Massachusetts residents add 5% sales tax.)

GIFT ORDERS:

If you would like   **Name** _____
this book sent to   **Address** _____
a name and   **City** _____
address other   **State/Zip** _____
than your own,
please specify:

                   Name _____

                   Address _____

                   City _____

                   State/Zip _____

                   Qty.   @

_____ $6.95   Total _____

Shipping and Handling _____

Massachusetts residents 5% sales tax _____

(Check or money order only) Total encl. _____